AYURVEDIC COOKBOOK FOR WESTERNERS

Discover the Healing Power of Ayurvedic Cuisine and Nourish your Body and Mind with Delicious and Healthy Recipes for the Modern Western Lifestyle

Elizabeth J. McKenzie

Copyright © 2023 by Elizabeth J. McKenzie

Table of Contents

INTRODUCTION

What is Ayurveda?

Ayurveda is a traditional system of medicine that originated in India more than 5,000 years ago. The word "Ayurveda" is derived from two Sanskrit words: "Ayur" meaning "life" and "Veda" meaning "science" or "knowledge". Ayurveda is considered to be the "science of life" and aims to promote health, prevent illness, and extend the human lifespan.

Ayurveda is based on the belief that health and wellness depend on a delicate balance between the mind, body, and spirit. This balance is achieved by maintaining the harmony between three fundamental energies or doshas: Vata, Pitta, and Kapha. These doshas represent the different physiological and psychological characteristics of an individual and are responsible for the body's functions, behaviors, and emotions.

Vata is the energy that controls movement, including bodily functions such as breathing, heartbeat, and nerve impulses. It is associated with the elements of air and ether and is thought to be the most unstable of the doshas. People with a predominance of Vata are usually thin, active, and have a quick mind.

Pitta is the energy that governs metabolism, including digestion and the body's ability to generate heat. It is associated with the elements of fire and water and is thought to be the most intense of the doshas. People with a predominance of Pitta are usually of medium build, have good digestion, and tend to be ambitious and competitive.

Kapha is the energy that governs structure, including the body's ability to store energy, maintain immunity and provide lubrication. It is associated with the elements of earth and water and is thought to be the most stable of the doshas. People with a predominance of Kapha are usually heavy, calm and have good endurance.

According to Ayurveda, when the doshas are in balance, the body is healthy and harmonious. However, when the doshas are out of balance, the body is susceptible to illness. Ayurveda believes that the cause of all illnesses is an imbalance in the doshas and that the key to good health is to restore and maintain this balance.

Ayurveda uses a variety of therapies to restore balance to the doshas, such as herbal medicine, massage, yoga, and meditation. Ayurvedic practitioners also place a strong emphasis on diet and lifestyle as a means of maintaining health and preventing illness.

Ayurveda encourages the consumption of whole, natural foods that are appropriate for the individual's dosha. For example, a person with a predominance of Vata should avoid foods that are dry, cold, or light, such as raw salads and crackers, and instead opt for warm, moist, and heavy foods, such as soups and stews.

Ayurveda also emphasizes the importance of eating according to the seasons. Eating seasonal foods that are grown locally is believed to provide the body with the necessary nutrients to adapt to the changing seasons, and thus maintain balance in the doshas. It also encourages a balanced lifestyle that includes regular exercise, adequate sleep, and the practice of yoga and meditation. These practices are believed to promote balance in the doshas, reduce stress, and improve overall well-being.

Ayurveda has been gaining popularity in the Western world in recent years as more and more people are looking for natural ways to improve their health and prevent illness. Ayurveda offers a holistic approach to health that emphasizes the importance of balance and harmony between the mind, body, and spirit. It is not just a system of medicine, but a way of life that aims to promote optimal health and well-being.

One of the key principles of Ayurveda is the concept of "prevention is better than cure". Ayurveda encourages individuals to take a proactive approach to their health, rather than waiting for illness to occur. This means that Ayurveda focuses on maintaining balance in the doshas, rather than just treating symptoms of illness.

Ayurveda also emphasizes the importance of individualized treatment. Every person is unique, and Ayurveda recognizes that what works for one person may not work for another. Ayurvedic practitioners take into account a person's individual dosha, symptoms, and lifestyle when developing a treatment plan.

Ayurveda is also known for its use of herbal medicine. Ayurvedic practitioners use a wide range of herbs and spices to treat a variety of conditions. These herbs are believed to have medicinal properties that can help to balance the doshas and promote health.

THE PRINCIPLES OF AYURVEDIC COOKING

The principles of Ayurvedic cooking are based on the belief that food is medicine and that the right combination of ingredients can help to balance the doshas and promote health. Ayurvedic cooking is all about using natural, whole foods, and traditional Ayurvedic spices to create meals that are both delicious and nutritious.

The first principle of Ayurvedic cooking is to use seasonal ingredients. Eating seasonal foods that are grown locally is believed to provide the body with the necessary nutrients to adapt to the changing seasons, and thus maintain balance in the doshas.

The second principle is to use whole, natural foods. Ayurveda encourages the consumption of whole, natural foods that are appropriate for the individual's dosha. This means avoiding processed and refined foods, and instead opting for foods that are as close to their natural state as possible.

The third principle is to use traditional Ayurvedic spices. Ayurveda recognizes the medicinal properties of certain herbs and spices, and believes that they can be used to balance the doshas and promote health. Some common Ayurvedic spices include turmeric, ginger, cumin, coriander, and black pepper.

The fourth principle is to use the right cooking methods. Ayurveda believes that the way food is cooked can affect its nutritional value and its ability to balance the doshas. Ayurvedic cooking methods include steaming, sautéing, and simmering, which are thought to be the best ways to preserve the nutritional value of food.

The fifth principle is to use the right combination of ingredients. Ayurveda believes that different foods have different properties and that they should be combined in the right way to balance the doshas and promote health. This means avoiding certain food combinations, such as mixing sweet and sour foods, and instead, pairing foods that complement each other.

In conclusion, the principles of Ayurvedic cooking are based on the belief that food is medicine and that the right combination of ingredients can help to balance the doshas and promote health. Ayurvedic cooking is all about using natural, whole foods, and traditional Ayurvedic spices to create meals that are both delicious and nutritious. It emphasizes the importance of using seasonal ingredients, whole, natural foods, traditional Ayurvedic spices, the right cooking methods, and the right combination of ingredients.

UNDERSTANDING YOUR AYURVEDIC BODY TYPE

Understanding your Ayurvedic body type, also known as dosha, is an important aspect of Ayurveda. The doshas represent the different physiological and psychological characteristics of an individual and are responsible for the body's functions, behaviors, and emotions.

There are three main doshas: **Vata**, **Pitta**, and **Kapha**. Each individual has a unique combination of doshas, known as their "dosha type" or "prakriti". The goal of Ayurveda is to understand and balance one's dosha type to promote optimal health and well-being.

Vata is the energy that controls movement, including bodily functions such as breathing, heartbeat, and nerve impulses. It is associated with the elements of air and ether and is thought to be the most unstable of the doshas. People with a predominance of **Vata** are usually thin, active, and have a quick mind. They tend to be easily excited, but also easily fatigued. They have a dry skin, and they tend to have trouble with constipation and insomnia.

Pitta is the energy that governs metabolism, including digestion and the body's ability to generate heat. It is associated with the elements of fire and water and is thought to be the most intense of the doshas. People with a predominance of **Pitta** are usually of medium build, have good digestion, and tend to be ambitious and competitive. They tend to have a strong appetite and a good digestion. They have a warm skin and they are prone to skin rashes, acne, and sunburns.

Kapha is the energy that governs structure, including the body's ability to store energy, maintain immunity and provide lubrication. It is associated with the elements of earth and water and is thought to be the most stable of the doshas. People with a predominance of **Kapha** are usually heavy, calm and have good endurance. They tend to have a good appetite, and they tend to have a good digestion. They have a cool skin and they tend to have trouble with weight gain, water retention, and sinus congestion.

There are several ways to understand your Ayurvedic body type, also known as dosha. Here are a few methods that can help you identify your dosha:

- Take an online quiz: There are many online quizzes available that can help you determine your dosha type. These quizzes typically ask questions about your physical and psychological characteristics, as well as your dietary and lifestyle habits.

- Consult an Ayurvedic practitioner: An Ayurvedic practitioner can perform a pulse analysis, physical examination, and take a detailed medical history to determine your dosha type. They can also provide personalized recommendations for diet, lifestyle, and other therapies to help balance your doshas.

- Self-assessment: You can also determine your dosha type by paying attention to your own physical and psychological characteristics. For example, if you tend to be thin, active, and easily excited, you may have a predominance of Vata. If you tend to be of medium build, ambitious, and have good digestion, you may have a predominance of Pitta. If you tend to be heavy, calm, and have good endurance, you may have a predominance of Kapha.

- Observe your physical symptoms: Pay attention to your physical symptoms such as skin type, digestion, sleep patterns, and energy levels. People with Vata dosha tend to have dry skin, constipation, and trouble sleeping, while those with Pitta tend to have sensitive skin, acid reflux, and a strong appetite. Kapha individuals tend to have oily skin, water retention, and a tendency towards weight gain.

- Consider your emotional and psychological characteristics: Notice your emotional and psychological characteristics, Vata individuals tend to be easily excited and easily fatigued, Pitta individuals tend to be ambitious and competitive, and Kapha individuals tend to be calm and have good endurance.

It's important to note that determining your Ayurvedic body type is not an exact science and it may take some trial and error to find the right balance for you. The key is to pay attention to your body's signals and make adjustments as needed. It's also important to seek the advice of an Ayurvedic practitioner to ensure that your self-assessment and observations are accurate and to help you balance your doshas.

It is important to note that every person has a unique combination of doshas, and that one's dosha type can also change throughout life due to factors such as age, diet, lifestyle, and stress levels. Ayurvedic practitioners use a variety of methods to determine an individual's dosha type, including pulse analysis, physical examination, and a detailed medical history.

THE BENEFITS OF AN AYURVEDIC DIET

An Ayurvedic diet is a holistic approach to eating that aims to balance the doshas and promote optimal health and well-being. There are several benefits of an Ayurvedic diet, including:

- Improving digestion: Ayurveda places a strong emphasis on the importance of good digestion, and an Ayurvedic diet is designed to support the digestive system by providing the body with the right balance of nutrients.

- Balancing the doshas: An Ayurvedic diet is tailored to the individual's dosha, which helps to balance the doshas and promote optimal health.

- Boosting immunity: Ayurvedic diets are rich in fruits, vegetables, and herbs that are high in antioxidants and other nutrients that support the immune system.

- Achieving and maintaining a healthy weight: An Ayurvedic diet is based on whole, natural foods and is designed to provide the body with the necessary nutrients without excess calories. This helps to achieve and maintain a healthy weight.

- Reducing stress: An Ayurvedic diet is designed to reduce stress by providing the body with the necessary nutrients to cope with stress.

- Improving skin health: An Ayurvedic diet is rich in fruits, vegetables, and nuts that provide the skin with the necessary nutrients to maintain its health.

- Providing energy: An Ayurvedic diet is designed to provide the body with the necessary nutrients to maintain energy levels throughout the day.

- Supporting the brain: An Ayurvedic diet is rich in fruits, vegetables, nuts, and seeds that provide the brain with the necessary nutrients to maintain optimal cognitive function.

HOW TO USE THIS COOKBOOK

Here are a few tips on how to use this cookbook:

Understand your dosha type: Before diving into the recipes, take the time to understand your Ayurvedic body type (dosha) and what foods and ingredients are best for you. This will help you choose recipes that will best support your health and well-being.

Plan your meals: Use the seasonal ingredient guide, meal planning and shopping list, and Ayurvedic lifestyle tips to plan your meals in advance. This will make it easier to stick to your Ayurvedic diet and ensure that you have all the ingredients you need on hand.

Try new ingredients: Ayurvedic cooking often uses ingredients that may be new to you. Don't be afraid to try new things, and experiment with different spices and herbs to find the flavors you like best.

Adjust the recipes to suit your taste: While the recipes in this cookbook are designed to balance the doshas, everyone's tastes are different. Feel free to make adjustments to the recipes to suit your own taste preferences.

Incorporate Ayurvedic principles into your daily life: Use the information in the book to incorporate Ayurvedic principles into your daily life. This includes not only the recipes but also the tips for meal planning, lifestyle, and understanding the impact of food attributes on the doshas.

Refer to the Glossary of Ayurvedic terms: Make use of the Glossary of Ayurvedic terms, which will help you understand the Ayurvedic terms used in the book and the Table of Contents which will help you navigate the book and find the recipes you're looking for quickly and easily.

In conclusion, this cookbook is designed to help you incorporate Ayurvedic principles into your daily life by providing you with delicious and nutritious recipes that are tailored to your individual dosha type. Use it as a guide and make adjustments as necessary to suit your own tastes and lifestyle.

CHAPTER 1: BREAKFAST RECIPES

Gluten-free Saffron & Walnut Bread

Ingredients:

- 1 cup gluten-free flour
- ½ cup almond flour
- ¼ cup walnuts, chopped
- ¼ teaspoon saffron
- 1 teaspoon baking powder
- ¼ teaspoon salt
- ¼ cup honey
- ¼ cup coconut oil, melted
- ½ cup almond milk
- 1 egg

Directions:

1. Preheat the oven to 350°F. Grease a loaf pan with coconut oil.
2. In a large mixing bowl, combine the gluten-free flour, almond flour, chopped walnuts, saffron, baking powder, and salt.
3. In a separate mixing bowl, mix together the honey, melted coconut oil, almond milk, and egg.
4. Add the wet ingredients to the dry ingredients and stir until well combined.

5. Pour the batter into the prepared loaf pan and bake for 20-25 minutes, or until a toothpick inserted into the center comes out clean.
6. Let the bread cool in the pan for 10 minutes before removing it and letting it cool completely on a wire rack.

Baked Apple with Rosemary

Ingredients:

- 2 apples, cored and sliced
- 1 tablespoon coconut oil
- 1 tablespoon honey
- 1 teaspoon rosemary, chopped
- ¼ teaspoon cinnamon
- ¼ teaspoon nutmeg

Directions:

1. Preheat the oven to 350°F. Grease a baking dish with coconut oil.
2. In a mixing bowl, combine the sliced apples, coconut oil, honey, rosemary, cinnamon, and nutmeg.
3. Toss the apple mixture until the apples are well coated.
4. Transfer the apples to the prepared baking dish and bake for 20-25 minutes, or until the apples are tender and lightly browned.

Sweet Potato Beet Hashbrowns with Scallions

Ingredients:

- 2 sweet potatoes, grated

- 1 beet, grated
- 1 tablespoon coconut oil
- ¼ teaspoon salt
- 2 scallions, chopped

Directions:

1. In a mixing bowl, combine the grated sweet potatoes and beets, coconut oil, and salt.
2. Heat a large skillet over medium heat. Once the skillet is hot, add the sweet potato and beet mixture and press down with a spatula to form a patty.
3. Cook the hashbrowns for about 5-7 minutes on each side, or until they are crispy and golden brown.
4. Once the hashbrowns are cooked, remove them from the skillet and place them on a plate.
5. Garnish the hashbrowns with the chopped scallions before serving.

Savory Corn Pancakes
Ingredients:

- 1 cup cornmeal
- ½ cup flour
- ½ teaspoon baking powder
- ¼ teaspoon salt
- ¼ teaspoon cumin
- ¼ teaspoon coriander
- ¼ teaspoon turmeric
- ½ cup almond milk
- 1 egg

- 2 tablespoons coconut oil

Directions:

1. In a mixing bowl, combine the cornmeal, flour, baking powder, salt, cumin, coriander, and turmeric.
2. In a separate mixing bowl, mix together the almond milk and egg.
3. Add the wet ingredients to the dry ingredients and stir until well combined.
4. Heat a skillet over medium heat. Once the skillet is hot, add 1 tablespoon of coconut oil.
5. Use a ladle to pour the batter onto the skillet and cook the pancakes for about 2-3 minutes on each side, or until they are golden brown and cooked through.
6. Repeat the process with the remaining batter, adding more coconut oil as needed.

Pumpkin Waffles with Pecan Maple Syrup

Ingredients:

- 1 cup flour
- ½ cup pumpkin puree
- ½ teaspoon baking powder
- ¼ teaspoon salt
- ¼ teaspoon cinnamon
- ¼ teaspoon nutmeg
- ½ cup almond milk
- 1 egg
- 2 tablespoons coconut oil
- ¼ cup pecans, chopped

- ¼ cup maple syrup

Directions:

1. In a mixing bowl, combine the flour, pumpkin puree, baking powder, salt, cinnamon, and nutmeg.
2. In a separate mixing bowl, mix together the almond milk and egg.
3. Add the wet ingredients to the dry ingredients and stir until well combined.
4. Preheat a waffle iron and grease with coconut oil.
5. Pour the batter into the waffle iron and cook for about 3-5 minutes, or until the waffles are golden brown and cooked through.
6. While the waffles are cooking, heat a small saucepan over medium heat. Add the chopped pecans and maple syrup, and stir until the pecans are lightly toasted and the syrup is heated through.
7. Once the waffles are done, remove them from the waffle iron and top with the pecan maple syrup before serving.

Mushroom Swiss Chard Frittata with Rosemary

Ingredients:

- 1 tablespoon coconut oil
- 1 onion, diced
- 1 cup mushrooms, sliced
- 2 cups swiss chard, chopped
- 6 eggs
- ¼ cup almond milk
- 1 teaspoon rosemary, chopped

- ¼ teaspoon salt
- ¼ teaspoon pepper

Directions:

1. Preheat the oven to 350°F. Grease a baking dish with coconut oil.
2. In a skillet, heat the coconut oil over medium heat. Add the diced onion and cook for about 2-3 minutes, or until softened.
3. Add the sliced mushrooms and chopped swiss chard to the skillet and continue to cook for about 5-7 minutes, or until the vegetables are tender.
4. In a mixing bowl, whisk together the eggs, almond milk, rosemary, salt, and pepper.
5. Add the cooked vegetables to the egg mixture and stir until well combined.
6. Pour the mixture into the prepared baking dish and bake for about20-25 minutes, or until the frittata is set and golden brown on top.
7. Let the frittata cool for a few minutes before slicing and serving.

Quinoa, Walnut & Date Warm Cereal

Ingredients:

- 1 cup quinoa
- 2 cups water
- ¼ teaspoon salt
- ¼ cup walnuts, chopped
- ¼ cup dates, chopped
- ¼ teaspoon cinnamon

- ¼ cup almond milk
- 1 tablespoon honey

Directions:

1. In a saucepan, combine the quinoa, water, and salt. Bring to a boil, then reduce the heat to low and cover the saucepan.
2. Cook for about 15-20 minutes, or until the quinoa is tender and the water is absorbed.
3. Remove the saucepan from the heat and add the chopped walnuts, dates, and cinnamon. Stir until well combined.
4. Serve the quinoa mixture in bowls and top with almond milk and honey before serving.

Grapefruit with Honey, Ginger & Cardamom

Ingredients:

- 2 grapefruits
- 1 tablespoon honey
- 1 teaspoon grated ginger
- ¼ teaspoon cardamom

Directions:

1. Cut the grapefruits in half and remove the segments.
2. In a small mixing bowl, combine the honey, grated ginger, and cardamom.
3. Spoon the mixture over the grapefruit segments and enjoy.

Greens & Fresh Herb Frittata

Ingredients:

- 1 tablespoon coconut oil
- 1 onion, diced
- 2 cups mixed greens (spinach, kale, arugula)
- ¼ cup fresh herbs (parsley, basil, cilantro)
- 6 eggs
- ¼ cup almond milk
- ¼ teaspoon salt
- ¼ teaspoon pepper

Directions:

1. Preheat the oven to 350°F. Grease a baking dish with coconut oil.
2. In a skillet, heat the coconut oil over medium heat. Add the diced onion and cook for about 2-3 minutes, or until softened.
3. Add the mixed greens and fresh herbs to the skillet and continue to cook for about 5-7 minutes, or until the vegetables are wilted.
4. In a mixing bowl, whisk together the eggs, almond milk, salt, and pepper.
5. Add the cooked greens and herbs to the egg mixture and stir until well combined.
6. Pour the mixture into the prepared baking dish and bake for about 20-25 minutes, or until the frittata is set and golden brown on top.
7. Let the frittata cool for a few minutes before slicing and serving.

Roasted Coconut Sesame Oatmeal
Ingredients:

- 1 cup rolled oats
- ½ cup shredded coconut
- 2 tbsp sesame seeds
- ¼ tsp salt
- 1 cup water or milk (dairy or non-dairy)
- 1 tbsp ghee or coconut oil
- 2 tbsp honey (optional)

Instructions:

1. Preheat the oven to 375°F.
2. In a large bowl, mix together the oats, shredded coconut, sesame seeds, and salt.
3. Spread the mixture onto a baking sheet and roast for 10-15 minutes, or until the oats are golden brown and fragrant.
4. In a medium saucepan, heat the water or milk and ghee or coconut oil over medium heat.
5. Stir in the roasted oats and bring to a boil.
6. Reduce the heat and let the oatmeal simmer for 5-7 minutes, or until it reaches your desired consistency.
7. Serve the oatmeal in bowls, and top with honey, if desired.

Cinnamon Oatmeal with Almonds & Milk

Ingredients:

- 1 cup rolled oats
- 1 cup milk (dairy or non-dairy)
- 1 tsp ground cinnamon
- ¼ tsp salt
- ¼ cup chopped almonds
- 1 tbsp honey (optional)

Instructions:

1. In a medium saucepan, bring the milk, cinnamon, and salt to a boil.
2. Stir in the oats and reduce the heat to low.
3. Cook the oatmeal for 5-7 minutes, or until it reaches your desired consistency.
4. Stir in the chopped almonds.
5. Serve the oatmeal in bowls and top with honey, if desired.

Roasted Rice with Dates, Cinnamon & Cardamom

Ingredients:

- 1 cup long-grain white or brown rice
- 2 cups water or broth
- 1 tsp ground cinnamon
- ¼ tsp ground cardamom
- ¼ tsp salt
- ¼ cup chopped dates
- 1 tbsp ghee or coconut oil

Instructions:

1. Preheat the oven to 375°F.
2. In a medium saucepan, bring the water or broth, cinnamon, cardamom, and salt to a boil.
3. Stir in the rice and reduce the heat to low.
4. Cover and simmer the rice for 18-20 minutes, or until the water is absorbed and the rice is tender.
5. Fluff the rice with a fork and stir in the chopped dates.

6. Spread the rice mixture onto a baking sheet and drizzle with ghee or coconut oil.
7. Roast the rice for 10-15 minutes, or until it is golden brown and fragrant.
8. Serve the rice in bowls and enjoy.

Chickpea Flour Pancakes with Spinach & Fennel
Ingredients:

- 1 cup chickpea flour
- ½ tsp ground cumin
- ¼ tsp salt
- ½ cup spinach, chopped
- ¼ cup fennel, finely chopped
- ½ cup water or milk (dairy or non-dairy)
- 1 tbsp ghee or coconut oil
- 1 tbsp honey (optional)

Instructions:

1. In a large bowl, mix together the chickpea flour, cumin, and salt.
2. Stir in the spinach, fennel, water or milk, and ghee or coconut oil.
3. Heat a non-stick skillet or griddle over medium heat.
4. Use a ¼ cup measuring cup to scoop the batter onto the skillet.
5. Cook the pancakes for 2-3 minutes on each side, or until they are golden brown and cooked through.
6. Serve the pancakes in a plate and top with honey, if desired.

Avocado Toast with Turmeric & Cumin

Ingredients:

- 2 slices of bread (gluten-free or whole-grain)
- 1 ripe avocado
- ½ tsp ground turmeric
- ½ tsp ground cumin
- ¼ tsp salt
- 1 tbsp lemon juice
- 1 tbsp ghee or coconut oil

Instructions:

1. Toast the bread slices to your desired level of crispness.
2. In a medium bowl, mash the avocado with a fork or a potato masher.
3. Stir in the turmeric, cumin, salt, and lemon juice.
4. Spread the avocado mixture on top of the toasted bread slices.
5. Heat a non-stick skillet or griddle over medium heat.
6. Cook the toast in the skillet or griddle for 2-3 minutes on each side, or until the bread is crispy and the avocado mixture is heated through.
7. Serve the toast in a plate and top with ghee or coconut oil.

Chia Pudding with Coconut Milk & Mango

Ingredients:

- 1 cup coconut milk
- ¼ cup chia seeds
- ¼ tsp ground cardamom
- ¼ tsp vanilla extract

- ¼ tsp salt
- ¼ cup diced fresh mango
- 1 tbsp honey (optional)

Instructions:

1. In a medium bowl, whisk together the coconut milk, chia seeds, cardamom, vanilla extract, and salt.
2. Cover the bowl and refrigerate for at least 2 hours or overnight.
3. Before serving, stir in the diced mango.
4. Serve the pudding in bowls and top with honey, if desired.

Vegetable Frittata with Turmeric & Cumin

Ingredients:

- 8 eggs
- ¼ cup milk (dairy or non-dairy)
- ¼ tsp ground turmeric
- ¼ tsp ground cumin
- ¼ tsp salt
- ¼ cup diced vegetables (such as bell peppers, onions, and tomatoes)
- 1 tbsp ghee or coconut oil

Instructions:

1. In a large bowl, whisk together the eggs, milk, turmeric, cumin, and salt.
2. Heat a non-stick skillet or griddle over medium heat.

3. Add the ghee or coconut oil and the diced vegetables to the skillet.
4. Sauté the vegetables for 2-3 minutes, or until they are tender.
5. Pour the egg mixture over the vegetables and cook for 5-7 minutes, or until the eggs are set.
6. Flip the frittata and cook for an additional 2-3 minutes.
7. Serve the frittata in a plate and Enjoy hot.

Spiced Yogurt with Honey & Cardamom
Ingredients:

- 1 cup plain yogurt (dairy or non-dairy)
- ¼ tsp ground cardamom
- ¼ tsp ground cinnamon
- 1 tbsp honey (optional)

Instructions:

1. In a medium bowl, mix together the yogurt, cardamom, and cinnamon.
2. Serve the yogurt in bowls and top with honey, if desired.

Baked Eggs with Spinach & Tomatoes
Ingredients:

- 4 eggs
- ¼ cup milk (dairy or non-dairy)
- ¼ tsp salt
- ¼ tsp black pepper
- ¼ cup chopped spinach
- ¼ cup diced tomatoes

- 1 tbsp ghee or coconut oil

Instructions:

1. Preheat the oven to 375°F.
2. In a large bowl, whisk together the eggs, milk, salt, and pepper.
3. Stir in the spinach and diced tomatoes.
4. Heat a non-stick skillet or griddle over medium heat.
5. Add the ghee or coconut oil to the skillet and pour in the egg mixture.
6. Cook the eggs for 2-3 minutes, or until the edges begin to set.
7. Transfer the skillet or griddle to the oven and bake for 5-7 minutes, or until the eggs are cooked through.
8. Serve the eggs in a plate and enjoy hot.

Turmeric & Cumin Scrambled Eggs with Spinach & Tomatoes

Ingredients:

- 4 eggs
- ¼ cup milk (dairy or non-dairy)
- ¼ tsp ground turmeric
- ¼ tsp ground cumin
- ¼ tsp salt
- ¼ cup chopped spinach
- ¼ cup diced tomatoes
- 1 tbsp ghee or coconut oil

Instructions:

1. In a large bowl, whisk together the eggs, milk, turmeric, cumin, and salt.
2. Heat a non-stick skillet or griddle over medium heat.
3. Add the ghee or coconut oil to the skillet and pour in the egg mixture.
4. Cook the eggs for 2-3 minutes, or until the edges begin to set.
5. Stir in the spinach and diced tomatoes and continue to cook for an additional 2-3 minutes, or until the eggs are cooked through.
6. Serve the eggs in a plate and enjoy hot.

CHAPTER 2: SOUPS AND SALADS

Spiced Lentil Soup With Ginger & Cumin

Ingredients:

- 2 cups of lentils
- 4 cups of vegetable broth
- 2 cups of water
- 2 tbsp of olive oil
- 1 onion, diced
- 2 cloves of garlic, minced
- 1 inch of ginger, grated
- 2 tsp of ground cumin
- Salt and pepper to taste
- Fresh cilantro for garnish

Instructions:

1. In a large pot, add the lentils, vegetable broth, and water. Bring to a boil, then reduce the heat and let simmer for about 30 minutes or until the lentils are soft.
2. In a separate pan, heat the olive oil and add the onion, garlic, and ginger. Cook until softened, about 5 minutes.
3. Add the cooked onion mixture and cumin to the pot of lentils, and cook for an additional 10 minutes.
4. Season with salt and pepper to taste.
5. Serve the soup in bowls, and garnish with fresh cilantro.

Roasted Vegetable & Quinoa Salad With Lemon & Mint
Ingredients:

- 2 cups of quinoa, cooked
- 2 cups of mixed vegetables (such as bell peppers, zucchini, and eggplant), roasted
- 2 tbsp of olive oil
- Juice of 1 lemon
- 2 tbsp of fresh mint, chopped
- Salt and pepper to taste

Instructions:

1. Preheat the oven to 400°F.
2. Toss the mixed vegetables with olive oil, salt, and pepper. Roast for 20-25 minutes or until tender.
3. In a large bowl, combine the cooked quinoa, roasted vegetables, lemon juice, and mint.
4. Season with salt and pepper to taste.
5. Serve the salad in bowls and enjoy!

Carrot & Ginger Soup With Lime & Cilantro
Ingredients:

- 2 cups of carrots, peeled and diced
- 4 cups of vegetable broth
- 2 cups of water
- 2 tbsp of olive oil
- 1 onion, diced
- 2 cloves of garlic, minced

- 1 inch of ginger, grated
- Juice of 1 lime
- Salt and pepper to taste
- Fresh cilantro for garnish

Instructions:

1. In a large pot, add the carrots, vegetable broth, and water. Bring to a boil, then reduce the heat and let simmer for about 30 minutes or until the carrots are soft.
2. In a separate pan, heat the olive oil and add the onion, garlic, and ginger. Cook until softened, about5 minutes.
3. Add the cooked onion mixture, lime juice, and cilantro to the pot of carrots and cook for an additional 10 minutes.
4. Season with salt and pepper to taste.
5. Use an immersion blender or a regular blender to puree the soup until smooth.
6. Serve the soup in bowls, and garnish with fresh cilantro.

Tomato & Cucumber Salad With Mint & Lime

Ingredients:

- 2 cups of tomatoes, diced
- 2 cups of cucumbers, diced
- 2 tbsp of olive oil
- Juice of 1 lime
- 2 tbsp of fresh mint, chopped
- Salt and pepper to taste

Instructions:

1. In a large bowl, combine the tomatoes, cucumbers, olive oil, lime juice, and mint.
2. Season with salt and pepper to taste.
3. Serve the salad in bowls and enjoy!

Sweet Potato & Lentil Soup With Turmeric & Ginger
Ingredients:

- 2 cups of lentils
- 4 cups of vegetable broth
- 2 cups of water
- 2 tbsp of olive oil
- 1 onion, diced
- 2 cloves of garlic, minced
- 1 inch of ginger, grated
- 2 tsp of ground turmeric
- Salt and pepper to taste
- Fresh cilantro for garnish

Instructions:

1. In a large pot, add the lentils, vegetable broth, and water. Bring to a boil, then reduce the heat and let simmer for about 30 minutes or until the lentils are soft.
2. In a separate pan, heat the olive oil and add the onion, garlic, and ginger. Cook until softened, about 5 minutes.
3. Add the cooked onion mixture, sweet potatoes, and turmeric to the pot of lentils and cook for an additional 10 minutes.
4. Season with salt and pepper to taste.
5. Use an immersion blender or a regular blender to puree the soup until smooth.

6. Serve the soup in bowls, and garnish with fresh cilantro.

Kale & Beet Salad With Lemon & Peppercorn Dressing

Ingredients:

- 2 cups of kale, chopped
- 2 cups of beets, roasted and diced
- 2 tbsp of olive oil
- Juice of 1 lemon
- 1 tsp of black peppercorns, crushed
- Salt and pepper to taste

Instructions:

1. In a large bowl, combine the kale, beets, olive oil, lemon juice, and crushed peppercorns.
2. Season with salt and pepper to taste.
3. Serve the salad in bowls and enjoy!

Coconut Milk & Lentil Soup With Cilantro & Lemongrass

Ingredients:

- 2 cups of lentils
- 4 cups of vegetable broth
- 2 cups of coconut milk
- 2 tbsp of olive oil
- 1 onion, diced
- 2 cloves of garlic, minced
- 1 inch of lemongrass, minced
- Salt and pepper to taste
- Fresh cilantro for garnish

Instructions:

1. In a large pot, add the lentils, vegetable broth, and coconut milk. Bring to a boil, then reduce the heat and let simmer for about 30 minutes or until the lentils are soft.
2. In a separate pan, heat the olive oil and add the onion, garlic, and lemongrass. Cook until softened, about 5 minutes.
3. Add the cooked onion mixture to the pot of lentils, and cook for an additional 10 minutes.
4. Season with salt and pepper to taste.
5. Use an immersion blender or a regular blender to puree the soup until smooth.
6. Serve the soup in bowls, and garnish with fresh cilantro.

Roasted Cauliflower & Chickpea Salad With Tahini Dressing
Ingredients:

- 2 cups of cauliflower, roasted
- 2 cups of chickpeas
- 2 tbsp of tahini
- Juice of 1 lemon
- 2 cloves of garlic, minced
- Salt and pepper to taste

Instructions:

1. Preheat the oven to 400°F.
2. Toss the cauliflower with olive oil, salt, and pepper. Roast for 20-25 minutes or until tender.
3. In a large bowl, combine the roasted cauliflower, chickpeas, tahini, lemon juice, and garlic.

4. Season with salt and pepper to taste.
5. Serve the salad in bowls and enjoy!

Chickpea & Spinach Soup With Cumin & Coriander
Ingredients:

- 2 cups of chickpeas, cooked
- 4 cups of vegetable broth
- 2 cups of spinach, chopped
- 2 tbsp of olive oil
- 1 onion, diced
- 2 cloves of garlic, minced
- 2 tsp of ground cumin
- 2 tsp of ground coriander
- Salt and pepper to taste
- Fresh cilantro for garnish

Instructions:

1. In a large pot, add the chickpeas, vegetable broth, and spinach. Bring to a boil, then reduce the heat and let simmer for about 15 minutes.
2. In a separate pan, heat the olive oil and add the onion, garlic, cumin, and coriander. Cook until softened, about 5 minutes.
3. Add the cooked onion mixture to the pot of chickpeas and spinach, and cook for an additional 10 minutes.
4. Season with salt and pepper to taste.
5. Use an immersion blender or a regular blender to puree the soup until smooth.
6. Serve the soup in bowls, and garnish with fresh cilantro.

Roasted Vegetable & Quinoa Salad With Avocado & Lime Dressing

Ingredients:

- 2 cups of quinoa, cooked
- 2 cups of mixed vegetables (such as bell peppers, zucchini, and eggplant), roasted
- 1 avocado, diced
- 2 tbsp of olive oil
- Juice of 1 lime
- Salt and pepper to taste

Instructions:

1. Preheat the oven to 400°F.
2. Toss the mixed vegetables with olive oil, salt, and pepper. Roast for 20-25 minutes or until tender.
3. In a large bowl, combine the cooked quinoa, roasted vegetables, avocado, lime juice, and olive oil.
4. Season with salt and pepper to taste.
5. Serve the salad in bowls and enjoy!

Coconut Milk & Vegetable Soup With Lemongrass & Ginger

Ingredients:

- 2 cups of mixed vegetables (such as bell peppers, zucchini, and eggplant)
- 4 cups of vegetable broth
- 2 cups of coconut milk
- 2 tbsp of olive oil
- 1 onion, diced
- 2 cloves of garlic, minced
- 1 inch of ginger, grated

- 1 inch of lemongrass, minced
- Salt and pepper to taste
- Fresh cilantro for garnish

Instructions:

1. In a large pot, add the vegetables, vegetable broth, and coconut milk. Bring to a boil, then reduce the heat and let simmer for about 30 minutes or until the vegetables are soft.
2. In a separate pan, heat the olive oil and add the onion, garlic, ginger, and lemongrass. Cook until softened, about 5 minutes.
3. Add the cooked onion mixture to the pot of vegetables, and cook for an additional 10 minutes.
4. Season with salt and pepper to taste.
5. Use an immersion blender or a regular blender to puree the soup until smooth.
6. Serve the soup in bowls, and garnish with fresh cilantro.

Roasted Broccoli & Chickpea Salad With Lemon & Parsley Dressing

Ingredients:

- 2 cups of broccoli, roasted
- 2 cups of chickpeas
- 2 tbsp of olive oil
- Juice of 1 lemon
- 2 tbsp of parsley, chopped
- Salt and pepper to taste

Instructions:

1. Preheat the oven to 400°F.
2. Toss the broccoli with olive oil, salt, and pepper. Roast for 20-25 minutes or until tender.
3. In a large bowl, combine the roasted broccoli, chickpeas, lemon juice, parsley, and olive oil.
4. Season with salt and pepper to taste.
5. Serve the salad in bowls and enjoy!

Lentil & Vegetable Soup With Turmeric & Cumin

Ingredients:

- 2 cups of lentils
- 4 cups of vegetable broth
- 2 cups of mixed vegetables (such as bell peppers, zucchini, and eggplant)
- 2 tbsp of olive oil
- 1 onion, diced
- 2 cloves of garlic, minced
- 2 tsp of ground turmeric
- 2 tsp of ground cumin
- Salt and pepper to taste
- Fresh cilantro for garnish

Instructions:

1. In a large pot, add the lentils, vegetable broth, and vegetables. Bring to a boil, then reduce the heat and let simmer for about 30 minutes or until the lentils and vegetables are soft.
2. In a separate pan, heat the olive oil and add the onion, garlic, turmeric, and cumin. Cook until softened, about 5 minutes.

3. Add the cooked onion mixture to the pot of lentils and vegetables, and cook for an additional 10 minutes.
4. Season with salt and pepper to taste.
5. Use an immersion blender or a regular blender to puree the soup until smooth.
6. Serve the soup in bowls, and garnish with fresh cilantro.

Roasted Carrot & Fennel Salad With Orange & Parsley Dressing
Ingredients:

- 2 cups of carrots, roasted
- 2 cups of fennel, sliced
- 2 tbsp of olive oil
- Juice of 1 orange
- 2 tbsp of parsley, chopped
- Salt and pepper to taste

Instructions:

1. Preheat the oven to 400°F.
2. Toss the carrots with olive oil, salt, and pepper. Roast for 20-25 minutes or until tender.
3. In a large bowl, combine the roasted carrots, fennel, orange juice, parsley, and olive oil.
4. Season with salt and pepper to taste.
5. Serve the salad in bowls and enjoy!

Split Pea Soup With Ginger & Turmeric
Ingredients:

- 2 cups of split peas

- 4 cups of vegetable broth
- 2 cups of mixed vegetables (such as bell peppers, zucchini, and eggplant)
- 2 tbsp of olive oil
- 1 onion, diced
- 2 cloves of garlic, minced
- 2 tsp of ground ginger
- 2 tsp of ground turmeric
- Salt and pepper to taste
- Fresh cilantro for garnish

Instructions:

1. In a large pot, add the split peas, vegetable broth, and vegetables. Bring to a boil, then reduce the heat and let simmer for about 30 minutes or until the split peas and vegetables are soft.
2. In a separate pan, heat the olive oil and add the onion, garlic, ginger, and turmeric. Cook until softened, about 5 minutes.
3. Add the cooked onion mixture to the pot of split peas and vegetables, and cook for an additional 10 minutes.
4. Season with salt and pepper to taste.
5. Use an immersion blender or a regular blender to puree the soup until smooth.
6. Serve the soup in bowls, and garnish with fresh cilantro.

Roasted Sweet Potato & Chickpea Salad With Cumin & Lime Dressing

Ingredients:

- 2 sweet potatoes, peeled and diced
- 1 can chickpeas, drained and rinsed

- 2 tbsp olive oil
- 1 tsp cumin powder
- Salt and pepper to taste
- ¼ cup cilantro, chopped
- 1 lime, juiced

Instructions:

1. Preheat the oven to 375F.
2. In a mixing bowl, toss the sweet potatoes, chickpeas, olive oil, cumin powder, salt, and pepper.
3. Spread the mixture on a baking sheet and roast for 20-25 minutes or until the sweet potatoes are cooked through.
4. In a serving bowl, combine the roasted sweet potatoes and chickpeas with the cilantro and lime juice.
5. Serve and enjoy!

Coconut Milk & Lentil Soup With Cumin & Coriander

Ingredients:

- 1 cup red lentils, rinsed
- 4 cups vegetable broth
- 1 can coconut milk
- 1 tbsp cumin powder
- 1 tsp coriander powder
- Salt and pepper to taste
- 1 tbsp olive oil
- 1 onion, diced
- 2 cloves garlic, minced
- 1 tsp grated ginger
- 1 tbsp cilantro, chopped (for garnish)

Instructions:

1. In a large pot, bring the lentils, vegetable broth, and coconut milk to a boil.
2. Reduce the heat and add the cumin powder, coriander powder, salt and pepper to the pot.
3. In a separate pan, heat the olive oil and sauté the onion, garlic, and ginger until softened.
4. Add the sautéed mixture to the pot with the lentils and let simmer for 20-25 minutes or until the lentils are cooked through.
5. Use an immersion blender to blend the soup until smooth.
6. Serve the soup in bowls, garnished with cilantro, and enjoy!

Roasted Vegetable & Quinoa Salad With Tahini & Lemon Dressing

Ingredients:

- 1 cup quinoa, rinsed
- 1 red bell pepper, diced
- 1 zucchini, diced
- 1 eggplant, diced
- 2 tbsp olive oil
- Salt and pepper to taste
- ¼ cup parsley, chopped
- 2 tbsp tahini
- 1 lemon, juiced
- 2 cloves of garlic, minced

Instructions:

1. Preheat the oven to 375F.

2. Cook the quinoa according to package instructions.
3. In a mixing bowl, toss the bell pepper, zucchini, eggplant, olive oil, salt, and pepper.
4. Spread the mixture on a baking sheet and roast for 20-25 minutes or until the vegetables are cooked through.
5. In a serving bowl, combine the cooked quinoa, roasted vegetables, and parsley.
6. In a separate mixing bowl, combine the tahini, lemon juice, garlic, salt and pepper. Whisk until smooth.
7. Drizzle the dressing over the salad, toss to combine and enjoy!

Vegetable & Lentil Soup With Cumin & Ginger

Ingredients:

- 1 cup green lentils, rinsed
- 4 cups vegetable broth
- 1 cup diced carrots
- 1 cup diced celery
- 1 cup diced onion
- 2 cloves garlic, minced
- 1 tsp grated ginger
- 1 tbsp cumin powder
- Salt and pepper to taste
- 2 tbsp olive oil

Instructions:

1. In a large pot, heat the olive oil and sauté the onion, garlic, and ginger until softened.
2. Add the cumin powder, salt and pepper, and stir to combine.

3. Add the lentils, vegetable broth, carrots, celery, and bring to a boil.
4. Reduce the heat and let simmer for 20-25 minutes or until the lentils and vegetables are cooked through.
5. Use an immersion blender to blend the soup until smooth.
6. Serve the soup in bowls and enjoy!

Roasted Cauliflower & Chickpea Salad With Lemon & Parsley Dressing

Ingredients:

- 1 head of cauliflower, cut into florets
- 1 can chickpeas, drained and rinsed
- 2 tbsp olive oil
- Salt and pepper to taste
- ¼ cup parsley, chopped
- 2 tbsp lemon juice
- 1 clove of garlic, minced

Instructions:

1. Preheat the oven to 375F.
2. In a mixing bowl, toss the cauliflower, chickpeas, olive oil, salt, and pepper.
3. Spread the mixture on a baking sheet and roast for 20-25 minutes or until the cauliflower is cooked through.
4. In a serving bowl, combine the roasted cauliflower and chickpeas with the parsley.
5. In a separate mixing bowl, combine the lemon juice, garlic, salt and pepper. Whisk until smooth.
6. Drizzle the dressing over the salad, toss to combine and enjoy!

CHAPTER 3: MAIN DISHES

Vegetable & Tofu Curry With Cumin & Coriander

Ingredients:

- 1 tablespoon olive oil or ghee
- 1 onion, finely chopped
- 2 cloves of garlic, minced
- 1 tablespoon cumin powder
- 1 teaspoon coriander powder
- 1 teaspoon turmeric powder
- 1 teaspoon paprika
- 1 teaspoon salt
- 1 cup mixed vegetables (carrots, bell peppers, zucchini, etc.)
- 1 cup cooked lentils
- 1 cup cubed tofu
- 1 cup coconut milk
- Fresh cilantro, for garnish

Instructions:

1. Heat the oil or ghee in a large pan over medium heat.
2. Add the onion and garlic, and sauté for 2-3 minutes or until softened.

3. Add the cumin, coriander, turmeric, paprika, and salt. Stir well.
4. Add the mixed vegetables and sauté for 5-7 minutes or until they start to soften.
5. Add the cooked lentils, tofu, and coconut milk. Stir well.
6. Reduce the heat to low, cover the pan and simmer for 15-20 minutes or until the vegetables are tender and the curry is thickened.
7. Garnish with fresh cilantro and serve hot with rice or quinoa.

Chicken Tikka Masala With Cumin & Ginger

Ingredients:

- 1 lb boneless chicken breast, cut into bite-size pieces
- 1 tablespoon olive oil or ghee
- 1 onion, finely chopped
- 2 cloves of garlic, minced
- 1 tablespoon grated ginger
- 1 tablespoon cumin powder
- 1 teaspoon coriander powder
- 1 teaspoon turmeric powder
- 1 teaspoon paprika
- 1 teaspoon salt
- 1 cup tomato puree
- 1 cup coconut milk
- Fresh cilantro, for garnish

Instructions:

1. Marinate the chicken in a mixture of yogurt, ginger, and spices for at least 30 minutes.

2. Heat the oil or ghee in a large pan over medium heat.
3. Add the onion and garlic, and sauté for 2-3 minutes or until softened.
4. Add the grated ginger and sauté for another minute.
5. Add the cumin, coriander, turmeric, paprika, and salt. Stir well.
6. Add the marinated chicken and sauté for 5-7 minutes or until the chicken is browned on all sides.
7. Add the tomato puree and coconut milk. Stir well.
8. Reduce the heat to low, cover the pan and simmer for 20-25 minutes or until the chicken is cooked through and the sauce is thickened.
9. Garnish with fresh cilantro and serve hot with rice or quinoa.

Lentil & Vegetable Stew With Turmeric & Cumin

Ingredients:

- 1 tablespoon olive oil or ghee
- 1 onion, finely chopped
- 2 cloves of garlic, minced
- 1 tablespoon grated ginger
- 1 teaspoon cumin powder
- 1 teaspoon turmeric powder
- 1 teaspoon coriander powder
- 1 teaspoon paprika
- 1 teaspoon salt
- 2 cups mixed vegetables (carrots, bell peppers, zucchini, etc.)
- 1 cup cooked lentils
- 1 cup vegetable broth
- Fresh cilantro, for garnish

Instructions:

1. Heat the oil or ghee in a large pan over medium heat.
2. Add the onion and garlic, and sauté for 2-3 minutes or until softened.
3. Add the grated ginger and sauté for another minute.
4. Add the cumin, turmeric, coriander, paprika, and salt. Stir well.
5. Add the mixed vegetables and sauté for 5-7 minutes or until they start to soften.
6. Add the cooked lentils, vegetable broth and bring to a simmer.
7. Reduce the heat to low, cover the pan and simmer for 15-20 minutes or until the vegetables are tender and the stew is thickened.
8. Garnish with fresh cilantro and serve hot with rice or quinoa.

Tofu & Vegetable Stir-Fry With Ginger & Lemongrass
Ingredients:

- 1 tablespoon olive oil or ghee
- 1 onion, finely chopped
- 2 cloves of garlic, minced
- 1 tablespoon grated ginger
- 1 teaspoon lemongrass paste
- 1 teaspoon cumin powder
- 1 teaspoon turmeric powder
- 1 teaspoon coriander powder
- 1 teaspoon salt
- 1 cup mixed vegetables (carrots, bell peppers, zucchini, etc.)
- 1 cup cubed tofu
- 1 tablespoon soy sauce

- 1 tablespoon rice vinegar
- Fresh cilantro, for garnish

Instructions:

1. Heat the oil or ghee in a large pan over medium heat.
2. Add the onion and garlic, and sauté for 2-3 minutes or until softened.
3. Add the grated ginger and lemongrass paste, sauté for another minute.
4. Add the cumin, turmeric, coriander and salt. Stir well.
5. Add the mixed vegetables and sauté for 5-7 minutes or until they start to soften.
6. Add the cubed tofu and stir-fry for another 2-3 minutes.
7. Add the soy sauce and rice vinegar and stir well.
8. Garnish with fresh cilantro and serve hot with rice or quinoa.

Chicken & Vegetable Curry With Cumin & Coriander

Ingredients:

- 1 lb boneless chicken breast, cut into bite-size pieces
- 1 tablespoon olive oil or ghee
- 1 onion, finely chopped
- 2 cloves of garlic, minced
- 1 tablespoon cumin powder
- 1 teaspoon coriander powder
- 1 teaspoon turmeric powder
- 1 teaspoon paprika
- 1 teaspoon salt
- 1 cup mixed vegetables (carrots, bell peppers, zucchini, etc.)
- 1 cup coconut milk

- Fresh cilantro, for garnish

Instructions:

1. Heat the oil or ghee in a large pan over medium heat.
2. Add the onion and garlic, and sauté for 2-3 minutes or until softened.
3. Add the cumin, coriander, turmeric, paprika, and salt. Stir well.
4. Add the chicken and sauté for 5-7 minutes or until it starts to brown.
5. Add the mixed vegetables and sauté for another 5-7 minutes or until they start to soften.
6. Add the coconut milk and bring to a simmer.
7. Reduce the heat to low, cover the pan and simmer for 15-20 minutes or until the chicken is cooked through and the curry is thickened.
8. Garnish with fresh cilantro and serve hot with rice or quinoa.

Vegetable & Tofu Korma With Cashew Cream
Ingredients:

- 1 tablespoon olive oil or ghee
- 1 onion, finely chopped
- 2 cloves of garlic, minced
- 1 tablespoon grated ginger
- 1 teaspoon cumin powder
- 1 teaspoon turmeric powder
- 1 teaspoon coriander powder
- 1 teaspoon paprika
- 1 teaspoon salt

- 2 cups mixed vegetables (carrots, bell peppers, zucchini, etc.)
- 1 cup cubed tofu
- 1 cup cashew cream
- Fresh cilantro, for garnish

Instructions:

1. Heat the oil or ghee in a large pan over medium heat.
2. Add the onion and garlic, and sauté for 2-3 minutes or until softened.
3. Add the grated ginger and sauté for another minute.
4. Add the cumin, turmeric, coriander, paprika, and salt. Stir well.
5. Add the mixed vegetables and sauté for 5-7 minutes or until they start to soften.
6. Add the cubed tofu and stir-fry for another 2-3 minutes.
7. Add the cashew cream and stir well.
8. Reduce the heat to low, cover the pan and simmer for 15-20 minutes or until the vegetables are tender and the korma is thickened.
9. Garnish with fresh cilantro and serve hot with rice or quinoa.

Quinoa & Vegetable Stir-Fry With Ginger & Lemongrass
Ingredients:

- 1 tablespoon olive oil or ghee
- 1 onion, finely chopped
- 2 cloves of garlic, minced
- 1 tablespoon grated ginger
- 1 teaspoon lemongrass paste
- 1 teaspoon cumin powder

- 1 teaspoon turmeric powder
- 1 teaspoon coriander powder
- 1 teaspoon salt
- 1 cup mixed vegetables (carrots, bell peppers, zucchini, etc.)
- 1 cup cooked quinoa
- 1 tablespoon soy sauce
- 1 tablespoon rice vinegar
- Fresh cilantro, for garnish

Instructions:

1. Heat the oil or ghee in a large pan over medium heat.
2. Add the onion and garlic, and sauté for 2-3 minutes or until softened.
3. Add the grated ginger and lemongrass paste, sauté for another minute.
4. Add the cumin, turmeric, coriander and salt. Stir well.
5. Add the mixed vegetables and sauté for 5-7 minutes or until they start to soften.
6. Add the cooked quinoa and stir-fry for another 2-3 minutes.
7. Add the soy sauce and rice vinegar and stir well.
8. Garnish with fresh cilantro and serve hot with additional quinoa or rice.

Chicken & Vegetable Stew With Turmeric & Cumin
Ingredients:

- 1 lb boneless chicken breast, cut into bite-size pieces
- 1 tablespoon olive oil or ghee
- 1 onion, finely chopped
- 2 cloves of garlic, minced

- 1 tablespoon grated ginger
- 1 teaspoon cumin powder
- 1 teaspoon turmeric powder
- 1 teaspoon coriander powder
- 1 teaspoon paprika
- 1 teaspoon salt
- 2 cups mixed vegetables (carrots, bell peppers, zucchini, etc.)
- 1 cup chicken broth
- Fresh cilantro, for garnish

Instructions:

1. Heat the oil or ghee in a large pan over medium heat.
2. Add the onion and garlic, and sauté for 2-3 minutes or until softened.
3. Add the grated ginger and sauté for another minute.
4. Add the cumin, turmeric, coriander, paprika, and salt. Stir well.
5. Add the chicken and sauté for 5-7 minutes or until it starts to brown.
6. Add the mixed vegetables and sauté for another 5-7 minutes or until they start to soften.
7. Add the chicken broth and bring to a simmer.
8. Reduce the heat to low, cover the pan and simmer for 15-20 minutes or until the chicken is cooked through and the stew is thickened.
9. Garnish with fresh cilantro and serve hot with rice or quinoa.

Tofu & Vegetable Curry With Cumin & Coriander
Ingredients:

- 1 tablespoon olive oil or ghee
- 1 onion, finely chopped
- 2 cloves of garlic, minced
- 1 tablespoon grated ginger
- 1 teaspoon cumin powder
- 1 teaspoon coriander powder
- 1 teaspoon turmeric powder
- 1 teaspoon paprika
- 1 teaspoon salt
- 2 cups mixed vegetables (carrots, bell peppers, zucchini, etc.)
- 1 cup cubed tofu
- 1 cup coconut milk
- Fresh cilantro, for garnish

Instructions:

1. Heat the oil or ghee in a large pan over medium heat.
2. Add the onion and garlic, and sauté for 2-3 minutes or until softened.
3. Add the grated ginger and sauté for another minute.
4. Add the cumin, coriander, turmeric, paprika, and salt. Stir well.
5. Add the mixed vegetables and sauté for 5-7 minutes or until they start to soften.
6. Add the cubed tofu and stir-fry for another 2-3 minutes.
7. Add the coconut milk and bring to a simmer.
8. Reduce the heat to low, cover the pan and simmer for 15-20 minutes or until the vegetables are tender and the curry is thickened.
9. Garnish with fresh cilantro and serve hot with rice or quinoa.

Vegetable & Lentil Stew With Ginger & Turmeric

Ingredients:

- 1 tablespoon olive oil or ghee
- 1 onion, finely chopped
- 2 cloves of garlic, minced
- 1 tablespoon grated ginger
- 1 teaspoon cumin powder
- 1 teaspoon turmeric powder
- 1 teaspoon coriander powder
- 1 teaspoon paprika
- 1 teaspoon salt
- 2 cups mixed vegetables (carrots, bell peppers, zucchini, etc.)
- 1 cup cooked lentils
- 1 cup vegetable broth
- Fresh cilantro, for garnish

Instructions:

1. Heat the oil or ghee in a large pan over medium heat.
2. Add the onion and garlic, and sauté for 2-3 minutes or until softened.
3. Add the grated ginger and sauté for another minute.
4. Add the cumin, turmeric, coriander, paprika, and salt. Stir well.
5. Add the mixed vegetables and sauté for 5-7 minutes or until they start to soften.
6. Add the cooked lentils, vegetable broth and bring to a simmer.
7. Reduce the heat to low, cover the pan and simmer for 15-20 minutes or until the vegetables are tender and the stew is thickened.

8. Garnish with fresh cilantro and serve hot with rice or quinoa.

Chicken & Vegetable Stir-Fry With Ginger & Lemongrass

Ingredients:

- 1 lb boneless chicken breast, cut into bite-size pieces
- 1 tablespoon olive oil or ghee
- 1 onion, finely chopped
- 2 cloves of garlic, minced
- 1 tablespoon grated ginger
- 1 teaspoon lemongrass paste
- 1 teaspoon cumin powder
- 1 teaspoon turmeric powder
- 1 teaspoon coriander powder1 teaspoon salt
- 2 cups mixed vegetables (carrots, bell peppers, zucchini, etc.)
- 1 tablespoon soy sauce
- 1 tablespoon rice vinegar
- Fresh cilantro, for garnish

Instructions:

1. Heat the oil or ghee in a large pan over medium heat.
2. Add the onion and garlic, and sauté for 2-3 minutes or until softened.
3. Add the grated ginger and lemongrass paste, sauté for another minute.
4. Add the cumin, turmeric, coriander and salt. Stir well.
5. Add the chicken and sauté for 5-7 minutes or until it starts to brown.
6. Add the mixed vegetables and sauté for another 5-7 minutes or until they start to soften.

7. Add the soy sauce and rice vinegar and stir well.
8. Garnish with fresh cilantro and serve hot with additional quinoa or rice.

Tofu & Vegetable Stew With Turmeric & Cumin

Ingredients:

- 1 tablespoon olive oil or ghee
- 1 onion, finely chopped
- 2 cloves of garlic, minced
- 1 tablespoon grated ginger
- 1 teaspoon cumin powder
- 1 teaspoon turmeric powder
- 1 teaspoon coriander powder
- 1 teaspoon paprika
- 1 teaspoon salt
- 2 cups mixed vegetables (carrots, bell peppers, zucchini, etc.)
- 1 cup cubed tofu
- 1 cup vegetable broth
- Fresh cilantro, for garnish

Instructions:

1. Heat the oil or ghee in a large pan over medium heat.
2. Add the onion and garlic, and sauté for 2-3 minutes or until softened.
3. Add the grated ginger and sauté for another minute.
4. Add the cumin, turmeric, coriander, paprika, and salt. Stir well.
5. Add the mixed vegetables and sauté for 5-7 minutes or until they start to soften.

6. Add the cubed tofu and stir-fry for another 2-3 minutes.
7. Add the vegetable broth and bring to a simmer.
8. Reduce the heat to low, cover the pan and simmer for 15-20 minutes or until the vegetables are tender and the stew is thickened.
9. Garnish with fresh cilantro and serve hot with rice or quinoa.

Vegetable & Lentil Curry With Cumin & Turmeric

Ingredients:

- 1 tablespoon olive oil or ghee
- 1 onion, finely chopped
- 2 cloves of garlic, minced
- 1 tablespoon grated ginger
- 1 teaspoon cumin powder
- 1 teaspoon turmeric powder
- 1 teaspoon coriander powder
- 1 teaspoon paprika
- 1 teaspoon salt
- 2 cups mixed vegetables (carrots, bell peppers, zucchini, etc.)
- 1 cup cooked lentils
- 1 cup coconut milk
- Fresh cilantro, for garnish

Instructions:

1. Heat the oil or ghee in a large pan over medium heat.
2. Add the onion and garlic, and sauté for 2-3 minutes or until softened.
3. Add the grated ginger and sauté for another minute.

4. Add the cumin, turmeric, coriander, paprika, and salt. Stir well.
5. Add the mixed vegetables and sauté for 5-7 minutes or until they start to soften.
6. Add the cooked lentils and stir-fry for another 2-3 minutes.
7. Add the coconut milk and bring to a simmer.
8. Reduce the heat to low, cover the pan and simmer for 15-20 minutes or until the vegetables are tender and the curry is thickened.
9. Garnish with fresh cilantro and serve hot with rice or quinoa.

Chicken & Vegetable Korma With Cashew Cream

Ingredients:

- 1 lb boneless chicken breast, cut into bite-size pieces
- 1 tablespoon olive oil or ghee
- 1 onion, finely chopped
- 2 cloves of garlic, minced
- 1 tablespoon grated ginger
- 1 teaspoon cumin powder
- 1 teaspoon turmeric powder
- 1 teaspoon coriander powder
- 1 teaspoon paprika
- 1 teaspoon salt
- 2 cups mixed vegetables (carrots, bell peppers, zucchini, etc.)
- 1 cup cashew cream
- Fresh cilantro, for garnish

Instructions:

1. Heat the oil or ghee in a large pan over medium heat.

2. Add the onion and garlic, and sauté for 2-3 minutes or until softened.
3. Add the grated ginger and sauté for another minute.
4. Add the cumin, turmeric, coriander, paprika, and salt. Stir well.
5. Add the chicken and sauté for 5-7 minutes or until it starts to brown.
6. Add the mixed vegetables and sauté for another 5-7 minutes or until they start to soften.
7. Add the cashew cream and stir well.
8. Reduce the heat to low, cover the pan and simmer for 10-15 minutes or until the chicken is cooked through and the vegetables are tender.
9. Garnish with fresh cilantro and serve hot with rice or quinoa.

Vegetable & Tofu Stir-Fry With Turmeric & Cumin

Ingredients:

- 1 tablespoon olive oil or ghee
- 1 onion, finely chopped
- 2 cloves of garlic, minced
- 1 tablespoon grated ginger
- 1 teaspoon cumin powder
- 1 teaspoon turmeric powder
- 1 teaspoon coriander powder
- 1 teaspoon salt
- 2 cups mixed vegetables (carrots, bell peppers, zucchini, etc.)
- 1 cup cubed tofu
- 1 tablespoon soy sauce
- 1 tablespoon rice vinegar
- Fresh cilantro, for garnish

Instructions:

1. Heat the oil or ghee in a large pan over medium heat.
2. Add the onion and garlic, and sauté for 2-3 minutes or until softened.
3. Add the grated ginger and sauté for another minute.
4. Add the cumin, turmeric, coriander, and salt. Stir well.
5. Add the mixed vegetables and sauté for 5-7 minutes or until they start to soften.
6. Add the cubed tofu and stir-fry for another 2-3 minutes.
7. Add the soy sauce and rice vinegar and stir well.
8. Garnish with fresh cilantro and serve hot with additional quinoa or rice.

CHAPTER 4: ENTREES

Lentil & Vegetable Stuffed Peppers with Cumin & Coriander
Ingredients:

- 1 cup red lentils, washed and drained
- 2 cups water
- 4 bell peppers, cut in half and seeded
- 2 tbsp olive oil
- 1 onion, diced
- 2 cloves of garlic, minced
- 1 tsp cumin powder
- 1 tsp coriander powder
- 1 tsp turmeric powder
- Salt and pepper, to taste
- Cilantro, for garnish

Instructions:

1. In a medium pot, bring lentils and water to a boil. Reduce heat and simmer for 20 minutes or until lentils are tender. Drain and set aside.
2. Preheat oven to 375F.
3. In a pan, heat olive oil over medium heat. Add onion and garlic and sauté for 2-3 minutes or until softened.
4. Add cumin, coriander, and turmeric powder and continue to sauté for another minute.

5. Add the cooked lentils to the pan and mix well. Season with salt and pepper to taste.
6. Stuff the lentil mixture into the bell pepper halves and place them in a baking dish.
7. Bake for 25-30 minutes or until the peppers are tender.
8. Garnish with cilantro and serve.

Chicken & Vegetable Samosas with Tamarind Chutney
Ingredients:

- 1 lb ground chicken
- 1 onion, diced
- 2 cloves of garlic, minced
- 1 tsp cumin powder
- 1 tsp coriander powder
- 1 tsp turmeric powder
- Salt and pepper, to taste
- 1 cup frozen mixed vegetables
- 1 package of store-bought samosa wrappers
- Oil, for frying
- Tamarind chutney, for dipping

Instructions:

1. In a pan, heat a little oil over medium heat. Add the ground chicken and cook until browned, about 5-7 minutes.
2. Add onion and garlic and sauté for 2-3 minutes or until softened.
3. Add cumin, coriander, and turmeric powder and continue to sauté for another minute.

4. Add the frozen vegetables and cook for an additional 5 minutes or until vegetables are tender.
5. Season with salt and pepper to taste.
6. Lay a samosa wrapper on a flat surface and spoon about 2 tablespoons of the chicken and vegetable mixture on one corner.
7. Roll the wrapper diagonally, making a cone shape, and seal the edges with a little water. Repeat with the remaining wrappers and filling.
8. Heat oil in a deep pan or wok over medium-high heat. Once hot, add the samosas and fry until they turn golden brown.
9. Remove the samosas from the oil and drain on a paper towel.
10. Serve the samosas with tamarind chutney for dipping.

Vegetable & Tofu Kofta With Ginger & Lemongrass

Ingredients:

- 1 block of firm tofu, drained and mashed
- 1 onion, diced
- 1 carrot, grated
- 1 cup frozen mixed vegetables
- 2 cloves of garlic, minced
- 1 inch piece of ginger, grated
- 1 lemongrass stalk, finely chopped
- 1 tsp cumin powder
- 1 tsp coriander powder
- Salt and pepper, to taste
- Oil, for frying
- Yogurt and mint chutney, for dipping

Instructions:

1. In a bowl, mix together the mashed tofu, onion, carrot, frozen vegetables, garlic, ginger, lemongrass, cumin powder, and coriander powder. Season with salt and pepper to taste.
2. Form the mixture into small balls or koftas.
3. Heat oil in a deep pan or wok over medium-high heat. Once hot, add the koftas and fry until they turn golden brown.
4. Remove the koftas from the oil and drain on a paper towel.
5. Serve the koftas with yogurt and mint chutney for dipping.

Chicken & Vegetable Kebabs with Cumin & Turmeric

Ingredients:

- 1 lb boneless chicken breast, cut into small cubes
- 1 onion, diced
- 1 cup frozen mixed vegetables
- 2 cloves of garlic, minced
- 1 tsp cumin powder
- 1 tsp turmeric powder
- Salt and pepper, to taste
- Skewers, soaked in water for 30 minutes
- Yogurt andmint chutney, for dipping

Instructions:

1. In a bowl, mix together the chicken cubes, onion, frozen vegetables, garlic, cumin powder, and turmeric powder. Season with salt and pepper to taste.
2. Thread the chicken and vegetable mixture onto skewers.
3. Heat a grill or grill pan to medium-high heat. Once hot, place the skewers on the grill and cook for 8-10 minutes, turning occasionally, or until the chicken is cooked through.

4. Serve the kebabs with yogurt and mint chutney for dipping.

Vegetable & Lentil Cutlets with Ginger & Cumin
Ingredients:

- 1 cup red lentils, washed and drained
- 2 cups water
- 2 tbsp olive oil
- 1 onion, diced
- 2 cloves of garlic, minced
- 1 inch piece of ginger, grated
- 1 tsp cumin powder
- 1 tsp coriander powder
- Salt and pepper, to taste
- Oil, for frying
- Yogurt and mint chutney, for dipping

Instructions:

1. In a medium pot, bring lentils and water to a boil. Reduce heat and simmer for 20 minutes or until lentils are tender. Drain and set aside.
2. In a pan, heat olive oil over medium heat. Add onion and garlic and sauté for 2-3 minutes or until softened.
3. Add ginger, cumin powder, and coriander powder and continue to sauté for another minute.
4. Add the cooked lentils to the pan and mix well. Season with salt and pepper to taste.
5. Form the mixture into small cutlets or patties.
6. Heat oil in a deep pan or wok over medium-high heat. Once hot, add the cutlets and fry until they turn golden brown.

7. Remove the cutlets from the oil and drain on a paper towel.
8. Serve the cutlets with yogurt and mint chutney for dipping.

Chicken & Vegetable Paratha with Yogurt & Mint Chutney

Ingredients:

- 1 lb boneless chicken breast, cut into small cubes
- 1 onion, diced
- 1 cup frozen mixed vegetables
- 2 cloves of garlic, minced
- 1 tsp cumin powder
- 1 tsp coriander powder
- Salt and pepper, to taste
- 1 package of store-bought paratha or roti
- Oil, for frying
- Yogurt and mint chutney, for dipping

Instructions:

1. In a pan, heat a little oil over medium heat. Add the chicken and cook until browned, about 5-7 minutes.
2. Add onion, garlic, cumin powder, and coriander powder and continue to sauté for another 2-3 minutes or until vegetables are tender.
3. Season with salt and pepper to taste.
4. Heat a pan or griddle over medium-high heat. Once hot, place the paratha on the pan and spoon some of the chicken and vegetable mixture on one half of the paratha.
5. Fold the other half of the paratha over the filling and press down gently.

6. Cook the paratha on both sides until it turns golden brown and crispy.
7. Serve the paratha with yogurt and mint chutney for dipping.

Vegetable & Tofu Pakoras with Cumin & Coriander
Ingredients:

- 1 block of firm tofu, drained and diced
- 1 onion, diced
- 1 cup frozen mixed vegetables
- 2 cloves of garlic, minced
- 2 tbsp besan (chickpea flour)
- 1 tsp cumin powder
- 1 tsp coriander powder
- Salt and pepper, to taste
- Oil, for frying
- Tamarind chutney, for dipping

Instructions:

1. In a bowl, mix together the diced tofu, onion, frozen vegetables, garlic, besan, cumin powder, and coriander powder. Season with salt and pepper to taste.
2. Form the mixture into small balls or pakoras.
3. Heat oil in a deep pan or wok over medium-high heat. Once hot, add the pakoras and fry until they turn golden brown.
4. Remove the pakoras from the oil and drain on a paper towel.
5. Serve the pakoras with tamarind chutney for dipping.

Chicken & Vegetable Jhalfrezi with Ginger & Lemongrass

Ingredients:

- 1 lb boneless chicken breast, cut into small cubes
- 1 onion, diced
- 1 cup frozen mixed vegetables
- 2 cloves of garlic, minced
- 1 inch piece of ginger, grated
- 1 lemongrass stalk, finely chopped
- 1 tsp cumin powder
- 1 tsp coriander powder
- 1 tsp turmeric powder
- Salt and pepper, to taste
- 1 tbsp oil
- Yogurt and mint chutney, for dipping

Instructions:

1. In a pan, heat oil over medium heat. Add chicken and cook until browned, about 5-7 minutes.
2. Add onion, garlic, ginger, lemongrass, cumin powder, coriander powder, and turmeric powder and continue to sauté for another 2-3 minutes or until vegetables are tender.
3. Season with salt and pepper to taste.
4. Reduce heat to low and let the mixture simmer for another 5-7 minutes.
5. Serve the jhalfrezi with yogurt and mint chutney for dipping.

Vegetable & Lentil Kofta Curry with Ginger & Lemongrass

Ingredients:

- 1 cup red lentils, washed and drained

- 2 cups water
- 2 tbsp oil
- 1 onion, diced
- 2 cloves of garlic, minced
- 1 inch piece of ginger, grated
- 1 lemongrass stalk, finely chopped
- 1 tsp cumin powder
- 1 tsp coriander powder
- 1 tsp turmeric powder
- Salt and pepper, to taste
- 1 cup coconut milk
- Yogurt and mint chutney, for dipping

Instructions:

1. In a medium pot, bring lentils and water to a boil. Reduce heat and simmer for 20 minutes or until lentils are tender. Drain and set aside.
2. In a pan, heat oil over medium heat. Add onion and garlic and sauté for 2-3 minutes or until softened.
3. Add ginger, lemongrass, cumin powder, coriander powder, and turmeric powder and continue to sauté for another minute.
4. Form the mixture into small balls or koftas.
5. Add the koftas to the pan and pour in the coconut milk. Bring the curry to a simmer.
6. Season with salt and pepper to taste.
7. Let the curry simmer for another 5-7 minutes or until the koftas are cooked through.
8. Serve the curry with yogurt and mint chutney for dipping.

Chicken & Vegetable Korma with Cashew Cream
Ingredients:

- 1 lb boneless chicken breast, cut into small cubes
- 1 onion, diced
- 1 cup frozen mixed vegetables
- 2 cloves of garlic, minced
- 1 inch piece of ginger, grated
- 1 tsp cumin powder
- 1 tsp coriander powder
- 1 tsp turmeric powder
- Salt and pepper, to taste
- 1 cup cashew cream
- Yogurt and mint chutney, for dipping

Instructions:

1. In a pan, heat a little oil over medium heat. Add the chicken and cook until browned, about 5-7 minutes.
2. Add onion, garlic, ginger, cumin powder, coriander powder, and turmeric powder and continue to sauté for another 2-3 minutes or until vegetables are tender.
3. Season with salt and pepper to taste.
4. Stir in the cashew cream and bring the mixture to a simmer.
5. Let the korma simmer for another 5-7 minutes or until the chicken is cooked through and the sauce thickens.
6. Serve the korma with yogurt and mint chutney for dipping.

Vegetable & Tofu Kathi Roll with Yogurt & Mint Chutney
Ingredients:

- 1 block of firm tofu, drained and diced

- 1 onion, diced1 cup frozen mixed vegetables
- 2 cloves of garlic, minced
- 1 tsp cumin powder
- 1 tsp coriander powder
- Salt and pepper, to taste
- 8-10 store-bought kathi rolls or parathas
- Oil, for frying
- Yogurt and mint chutney, for dipping

Instructions:

1. In a pan, heat a little oil over medium heat. Add the diced tofu and cook for 2-3 minutes or until it starts to brown.
2. Add onion, garlic, cumin powder, and coriander powder and continue to sauté for another 2-3 minutes or until vegetables are tender.
3. Season with salt and pepper to taste.
4. Heat a pan or griddle over medium-high heat. Once hot, place the kathi rolls or parathas on the pan and spoon some of the tofu and vegetable mixture on one half of the roll.
5. Fold the other half of the roll over the filling and press down gently.
6. Cook the roll on both sides until it turns golden brown and crispy.
7. Serve the kathi roll with yogurt and mint chutney for dipping.

Chicken & Vegetable Biryani with Cumin & Turmeric
Ingredients:

- 1 lb boneless chicken breast, cut into small cubes

- 1 onion, diced
- 1 cup frozen mixed vegetables
- 2 cloves of garlic, minced
- 1 inch piece of ginger, grated
- 2 cups basmati rice, washed and drained
- 1 tsp cumin powder
- 1 tsp turmeric powder
- Salt and pepper, to taste
- 3 cups chicken broth
- 1 tbsp oil
- Yogurt and mint chutney, for dipping

Instructions:

1. In a pan, heat oil over medium heat. Add chicken and cook until browned, about 5-7 minutes.
2. Add onion, garlic, ginger, cumin powder, and turmeric powder and continue to sauté for another 2-3 minutes or until vegetables are tender.
3. Season with salt and pepper to taste.
4. Stir in the rice and chicken broth and bring the mixture to a boil.
5. Reduce heat to low, cover the pan with a lid, and let the biryani simmer for 18-20 minutes or until the rice is cooked through and the liquid is absorbed.
6. Fluff the biryani with a fork and serve with yogurt and mint chutney for dipping.

Vegetable & Lentil Kofta Curry with Ginger & Cumin
Ingredients:

- 1 cup red lentils washed and drained
- 2 cups water
- 2 tbsp oil
- 1 onion, diced
- 2 cloves of garlic, minced
- 1 inch piece of ginger, grated
- 1 tsp cumin powder
- 1 tsp coriander powder
- 1 tsp turmeric powder
- Salt and pepper, to taste
- 2 cups tomato puree
- Yogurt and mint chutney, for dipping

Instructions:

1. In a medium pot, bring lentils and water to a boil. Reduce heat and simmer for 20 minutes or until lentils are tender. Drain and set aside.
2. In a pan, heat oil over medium heat. Add onion and garlic and sauté for 2-3 minutes or until softened.
3. Add ginger, cumin powder, coriander powder, and turmeric powder and continue to sauté for another minute.
4. Form the mixture into small balls or koftas.
5. Add the koftas to the pan and pour in the tomato puree. Bring the curry to a simmer.
6. Season with salt and pepper to taste.
7. Let the curry simmer for another 10-15 minutes or until the koftas are cooked through and the sauce thickens.
8. Serve the curry with yogurt and mint chutney for dipping.

Chicken & Vegetable Kofta with Cumin & Turmeric

Ingredients:

- 1 lb ground chicken
- 1 onion, diced
- 1 cup frozen mixed vegetables
- 2 cloves of garlic, minced
- 1 tsp cumin powder
- 1 tsp turmeric powder
- Salt and pepper, to taste
- Oil, for frying
- Yogurt and mint chutney, for dipping

Instructions:

1. In a large bowl, mix together ground chicken, onion, vegetables, garlic, cumin powder, turmeric powder, salt, and pepper.
2. Form the mixture into small balls or koftas.
3. Heat a pan or griddle over medium-high heat and add oil.
4. Once hot, add the koftas to the pan and cook for 3-4 minutes on each side or until golden brown and cooked through.
5. Serve the koftas with yogurt and mint chutney for dipping.

Vegetable & Tofu Kofta Curry with Ginger & Cumin

Ingredients:

- 1 block of firm tofu, drained and diced
- 1 onion, diced
- 1 cup frozen mixed vegetables
- 2 cloves of garlic, minced
- 1 inch piece of ginger, grated

- 1 tsp cumin powder
- 1 tsp coriander powder
- Salt and pepper, to taste
- 2 cups tomato puree
- Yogurt and mint chutney, for dipping

Instructions:

1. In a pan, heat a little oil over medium heat. Add the diced tofu and cook for 2-3 minutes or until it starts to brown.
2. Add onion, garlic, ginger, cumin powder, and coriander powder and continue to sauté for another 2-3 minutes or until vegetables are tender.
3. Season with salt and pepper to taste.
4. Form the mixture into small balls or koftas.
5. Add the koftas to the pan and pour in the tomato puree. Bring the curry to a simmer.
6. Let the curry simmer for another 10-15 minutes or until the koftas are cooked through and the sauce thickens.
7. Serve the curry with yogurt and mint chutney for dipping.

Chicken & Vegetable Kofta with Yogurt & Tamarind Chutney
Ingredients:

- 1 lb ground chicken
- 1 onion, diced
- 1 cup frozen mixed vegetables
- 2 cloves of garlic, minced
- 1 tsp cumin powder
- 1 tsp turmeric powder
- Salt and pepper, to taste

- Oil, for frying
- Yogurt and tamarind chutney, for dipping

Instructions:

1. In a large bowl, mix together ground chicken, onion, vegetables, garlic, cumin powder, turmeric powder, salt, and pepper.
2. Form the mixture into small balls or koftas.
3. Heat a pan or griddle over medium-high heat and add oil.
4. Once hot, add the koftas to the pan and cook for 3-4 minutes on each side or until golden brown and cooked through.
5. Serve the koftas with yogurt and tamarind chutney for dipping.

Vegetable & Tofu Kofta with Cumin & Coriander

Ingredients:

- 1 block of firm tofu, drained and diced
- 1 onion, diced
- 1 cup frozen mixed vegetables
- 2 cloves of garlic, minced
- 1 tsp cumin powder
- 1 tsp coriander powder
- Salt and pepper, to taste
- Oil, for frying
- Yogurt and mint chutney, for dipping

Instructions:

1. In a pan, heat a little oil over medium heat. Add the diced tofu and cook for 2-3 minutes or until it starts to brown.
2. Add onion, garlic, cumin powder, and coriander powder and continue to sauté for another 2-3 minutes or until vegetables are tender.
3. Season with salt and pepper to taste.
4. Form the mixture into small balls or koftas.
5. Heat a pan or griddle over medium-high heat and add oil.
6. Once hot, add the koftas to the pan and cook for 3-4 minutes on each side or until golden brown and cooked through.
7. Serve the koftas with yogurt and mint chutney for dipping.

Chicken & Vegetable Korma with Coconut Milk & Lemongrass
Ingredients:

- 1 lb boneless chicken breast, cut into small cubes
- 1 onion, diced
- 1 cup frozen mixed vegetables
- 2 cloves of garlic, minced
- 1 inch piece of ginger, grated
- 1 tsp cumin powder
- 1 tsp turmeric powder
- Salt and pepper, to taste
- 1 cup coconut milk
- 1 stalk of lemongrass, bruised
- Yogurt and mint chutney, for dipping

Instructions:

1. In a pan, heat oil over medium heat. Add chicken and cook until browned, about 5-7 minutes.

2. Add onion, garlic, ginger, cumin powder, turmeric powder, and lemongrass and continue to sauté for another 2-3 minutes or until vegetables are tender.
3. Season with salt and pepper to taste.
4. Stir in the coconut milk and bring the mixture to a simmer.
5. Let the korma simmer for another 10-15 minutes or until the chicken is cooked through and the sauce thickens.
6. Serve the korma with yogurt and mint chutney for dipping.

Vegetable & Lentil Stuffed Eggplant with Turmeric & Cumin

Ingredients:

- 1 cup red lentils, washed and drained
- 2 cups water
- 2 eggplants, cut in half lengthwise
- 2 tbsp oil
- 1 onion, diced
- 2 cloves of garlic, minced
- 1 inch piece of ginger, grated
- 1 tsp cumin powder
- 1 tsp turmeric powder
- Salt and pepper, to taste
- 2 cups tomato puree
- Yogurt and mint chutney, for dipping

Instructions:

1. In a medium pot, bring lentils and water to a boil. Reduce heat and simmer for 20 minutes or until lentils are tender. Drain and set aside.
2. Preheat the oven to 350°F.

3. Scoop out the flesh of the eggplant halves, leaving a ¼-inch border around the edges. Chop the flesh and set aside.

4. In a pan, heat oil over medium heat. Add onion and garlic and sauté for 2-3 minutes or until softened.

5. Add ginger, cumin powder, turmeric powder, and the chopped eggplant flesh and continue to sauté for another 2-3 minutes.

6. Mix in the cooked lentils and season with salt and pepper to taste.

7. Stuff the mixture into the eggplant halves and place them in a baking dish.

8. Pour tomato puree over the eggplants and cover the dish with foil.

9. Bake for 30-40 minutes or until the eggplants are tender.

10.   Serve the eggplants with yogurt and mint chutney for dipping.

Chicken & Vegetable Biryani with Cumin & Turmeric
Ingredients:

- 1 lb boneless chicken breast, cut into small cubes
- 1 onion, diced
- 1 cup frozen mixed vegetables
- 2 cloves of garlic, minced
- 1 tsp cumin powder
- 1 tsp turmeric powder
- Salt and pepper, to taste
- 1 cup basmati rice, rinsed and drained
- 2 cups water or chicken broth
- Yogurt and mint chutney, for dipping

Instructions:

1. In a pan, heat oil over medium heat. Add chicken and cook until browned, about 5-7 minutes.
2. Add onion, garlic, cumin powder, turmeric powder, and vegetables and continue to sauté for another 2-3 minutes or until vegetables are tender.
3. Season with salt and pepper to taste.
4. Add rice and stir to coat with the spices and vegetables.
5. Pour in water or chicken broth and bring the mixture to a simmer.
6. Reduce heat to low, cover, and let the biryani simmer for 18-20 minutes or until the rice is tender and the liquid is absorbed.
7. Serve the biryani with yogurt and mint chutney for dipping.

Vegetable & Tofu Kathi Roll with Yogurt & Mint Chutney

Ingredients:

- 1 block of firm tofu, drained and diced
- 1 onion, diced
- 1 cup frozen mixed vegetables
- 2 cloves of garlic, minced
- 1 tsp cumin powder
- 1 tsp coriander powder
- Salt and pepper, to taste
- 4-6 roti or chapati
- Yogurt and mint chutney, for dipping

Instructions:

1. In a pan, heat a little oil over medium heat. Add the diced tofu and cook for 2-3 minutes or until it starts to brown.
2. Add onion, garlic, cumin powder, and coriander powder and continue to sauté for another 2-3 minutes or until vegetables are tender.
3. Season with salt and pepper to taste.
4. Heat a griddle or pan over medium-high heat. Place one roti or chapati on the griddle and cook for 1-2 minutes or until heated through and slightly puffed.
5. Spread a spoonful of the tofu and vegetable mixture on one half of the roti, leaving a small border around the edges.
6. Fold the roti in half, enclosing the filling.
7. Repeat with the remaining roti and filling.
8. Serve the Kathi Rolls with yogurt and mint chutney for dipping.

Chicken & Vegetable Kofta with Yogurt & Mint Chutney

Ingredients:

- 1 lb ground chicken
- 1 onion, diced
- 1 cup frozen mixed vegetables
- 2 cloves of garlic, minced
- 1 tsp cumin powder
- 1 tsp turmeric powder
- Salt and pepper, to taste
- Oil, for frying
- Yogurt and mint chutney, for dipping

Instructions:

1. In a large bowl, mix together ground chicken, onion, vegetables, garlic, cumin powder, turmeric powder, salt, and pepper.
2. Form the mixture into small balls or koftas.
3. Heat a pan or griddle over medium-high heat and add oil.
4. Once hot, add the koftas to the pan and cook for 3-4 minutes on each side or until golden brown and cooked through.
5. Serve the koftas with yogurt and mint chutney for dipping.

Vegetable & Lentil Kofta Curry with Ginger & Cumin

Ingredients:

- 1 cup red lentils, washed and drained
- 2 cups water
- 1 onion, diced
- 2 cloves of garlic, minced
- 1 inch piece of ginger, grated
- 1 tsp cumin powder
- 1 tsp turmeric powder
- Salt and pepper, to taste
- 2 cups tomato puree
- Oil, for frying
- Yogurt and mint chutney, for dipping

Instructions:

1. In a medium pot, bring lentils and water to a boil. Reduce heat and simmer for 20 minutes or until lentils are tender. Drain and set aside.
2. In a pan, heat oil over medium heat. Add onion and garlic and sauté for 2-3 minutes or until softened.

3. Add ginger, cumin powder, turmeric powder and continue to sauté for another 2-3 minutes.
4. Mix in the cooked lentils and season with salt and pepper to taste.
5. Form the mixture into small balls or koftas.
6. Heat a pan or griddle over medium-high heat and add oil.
7. Once hot, add the koftas to the pan and cook for 3-4 minutes on each side or until golden brown and cooked through.
8. In a pan, add the tomato puree and bring to a simmer.
9. Add the koftas and let simmer for another 10-15 minutes or until the sauce thickens.
10. Serve the curry with yogurt and mint chutney for dipping.

Vegetable & Tofu Kofta with Ginger & Lemongrass

Ingredients:

- 1 block of firm tofu, drained and diced
- 1 onion, diced
- 1 cup frozen mixed vegetables
- 2 cloves of garlic, minced
- 1 inch piece of ginger, grated
- 1 tsp cumin powder
- 1 tsp turmeric powder
- Salt and pepper, to taste
- Oil, for frying
- 2 stalks of lemongrass, bruised and minced
- Yogurt and mint chutney, for dipping

Instructions:

1. In a pan, heat a little oil over medium heat. Add the diced tofu and cook for 2-3 minutes or until it starts to brown.
2. Add onion, garlic, ginger, cumin powder, turmeric powder, and vegetables and continue to sauté for another 2-3 minutes or until vegetables are tender.
3. Season with salt and pepper to taste.
4. Remove from heat and add the minced lemongrass to the mixture, stirring well to combine.
5. Form the mixture into small balls or koftas.
6. Heat a pan or griddle over medium-high heat and add oil.
7. Once hot, add the koftas to the pan and cook for 3-4 minutes on each side or until golden brown and cooked through.
8. Serve the koftas with yogurt and mint chutney for dipping.

Chicken & Vegetable Korma with Cashew Cream

Ingredients:

- 1 lb boneless chicken breast, cut into small cubes
- 1 onion, diced
- 1 cup frozen mixed vegetables
- 2 cloves of garlic, minced
- 1 tsp cumin powder
- 1 tsp turmeric powder
- Salt and pepper, to taste
- 1 cup cashews, soaked in water for 30 minutes
- 1 cup coconut milk
- Yogurt and mint chutney, for dipping

Instructions:

1. In a pan, heat oil over medium heat. Add chicken and cook until browned, about 5-7 minutes.
2. Add onion, garlic, cumin powder, turmeric powder, and vegetables and continue to sauté for another 2-3 minutes or until vegetables are tender.
3. Season with salt and pepper to taste.
4. Drain the soaked cashews and blend them with the coconut milk in a blender until smooth.
5. Pour the cashew cream into the pan and stir to combine with the chicken and vegetables.
6. Let the mixture simmer for another 10-15 minutes or until the sauce thickens.
7. Serve the korma with yogurt and mint chutney for dipping.

Chicken & Vegetable Kebabs with Cumin & Turmeric

Ingredients:

- 1 lb boneless chicken breast, cut into small cubes
- 1 onion, diced
- 1 cup frozen mixed vegetables
- 2 cloves of garlic, minced
- 1 tsp cumin powder
- 1 tsp turmeric powder
- Salt and pepper, to taste
- Oil, for brushing
- Yogurt and mint chutney, for dipping

Instructions:

1. In a large bowl, mix together chicken, onion, vegetables, garlic, cumin powder, turmeric powder, salt, and pepper.

2. Form the mixture into small kebabs.
3. Heat a grill or griddle over medium-high heat. Brush the kebabs with oil.
4. Grill the kebabs for 3-4 minutes on each side or until cooked through.
5. Serve the kebabs with yogurt and mint chutney for dipping.

CHAPTER 5: RELISHES AND SAUCES

Cumin & Coriander Roasted Sweet Potatoes with Scallions

- 2 medium sweet potatoes, peeled and diced
- 2 tablespoons olive oil
- 1 teaspoon cumin powder
- 1 teaspoon coriander powder
- Salt and pepper to taste
- 2 scallions, thinly sliced

Instructions:

1. Preheat oven to 375F.
2. In a large bowl, combine the sweet potatoes, olive oil, cumin powder, coriander powder, salt and pepper. Mix well.
3. Spread the sweet potato mixture on a baking sheet and bake for 20-25 minutes, or until tender.
4. Take out of the oven and toss with scallions. Serve warm.

Chickpea & Spinach Sauté with Lemon & Parsley

- 1 tablespoon olive oil
- 1 onion, diced
- 2 cloves of garlic, minced
- 1 teaspoon cumin powder
- 1 can of chickpeas, drained and rinsed
- 2 cups of spinach, washed and chopped

- Salt and pepper to taste
- Juice of 1 lemon
- 2 tablespoons chopped parsley

Instructions:

1. Heat the olive oil in a pan over medium heat.
2. Add the onion and garlic, sauté for 2-3 minutes.
3. Add the cumin powder, chickpeas and spinach, sauté for another 2-3 minutes.
4. Season with salt and pepper.
5. Add the lemon juice and parsley, toss to combine. Serve warm.

Lentil & Vegetable Dosa with Tamarind & Cilantro Chutney

- 1 cup lentils, soaked overnight
- 2 cups of mixed vegetables, diced (carrots, bell peppers, zucchini, etc.)
- 1 teaspoon cumin powder
- Salt and pepper to taste
- 1 cup of water
- 1 cup of Tamarind Chutney
- 2 tablespoons chopped cilantro

Instructions:

1. Drain the lentils and place them in a blender, add water and blend until smooth.
2. In a pan, sauté the vegetables with cumin powder, salt, and pepper.
3. Mix the vegetables with the lentils batter.

4. Heat a non-stick skillet over medium heat and pour a ladleful of the batter. Spread it out evenly.
5. Cook for 2-3 minutes or until the edges start to curl up.
6. Flip and cook for another 2-3 minutes.
7. Serve warm with Tamarind Chutney and cilantro.

Ayurvedic Trail Mix with Nuts, Seeds & Dried Fruits

Ingredients:

- 1 cup of almonds
- ½ cup of pumpkin seeds
- ½ cup of sunflower seeds
- ¼ cup of sesame seeds
- ¼ cup of flax seeds
- ½ cup of dried cranberries
- ½ cup of dried apricots
- ¼ cup of honey
- 1 teaspoon of cinnamon powder
- ¼ teaspoon of nutmeg powder

Instructions:

1. Preheat oven to 350F.
2. In a large mixing bowl, combine the almonds, pumpkin seeds, sunflower seeds, sesame seeds, flax seeds, dried cranberries, dried apricots, honey, cinnamon powder, and nutmeg powder. Mix well.
3. Spread the mixture on a baking sheet and bake for 10-15 minutes, or until golden brown.
4. Take out of the oven and let it cool.

5. Once cool, store in an airtight container. Enjoy as a snack or add to yogurt or oatmeal for added crunch.

Cumin & Turmeric Roasted Eggplant with Yogurt & Mint Chutney

Ingredients:

- 2 medium eggplants, sliced
- 2 tablespoons olive oil
- 1 teaspoon cumin powder
- 1 teaspoon turmeric powder
- Salt and pepper to taste
- 1 cup of plain yogurt
- 2 tablespoons mint chutney

Instructions:

1. Preheat oven to 375F.
2. In a large bowl, combine the eggplant slices, olive oil, cumin powder, turmeric powder, salt and pepper. Mix well.
3. Spread the eggplant mixture on a baking sheet and bake for 20-25 minutes, or until tender.
4. Take out of the oven and let it cool.
5. Serve warm, topped with a dollop of yogurt and mint chutney on top.

Spinach & Fenugreek Pesto with Walnuts & Lemon

Ingredients:

- 2 cups of spinach, washed and chopped
- 1 cup of fenugreek leaves, washed and chopped
- ½ cup of walnuts

- 2 cloves of garlic
- ¼ cup of olive oil
- Juice of 1 lemon
- Salt and pepper to taste

Instructions:

1. In a food processor, combine the spinach, fenugreek leaves, walnuts, garlic, olive oil, lemon juice, salt, and pepper. Pulse until smooth.
2. Taste and adjust seasoning as needed.
3. Store in an airtight container in the refrigerator for up to a week.
4. Serve with pasta, on sandwiches, or as a dip.

Lentil & Vegetable Raita with Cumin & Coriander
Ingredients:

- 1 cup of cooked lentils
- 2 cups of mixed vegetables, diced (cucumber, tomatoes, bell peppers)
- 1 cup of plain yogurt
- 1 teaspoon cumin powder
- 1 teaspoon coriander powder
- Salt and pepper to taste

Instructions:

1. In a large mixing bowl, combine the lentils, vegetables, yogurt, cumin powder, coriander powder, salt and pepper. Mix well.

2. Taste and adjust seasoning as needed.
3. Serve chilled as a side dish or as a dip with pita bread or crackers.

Ayurvedic Chutney with Tamarind, Ginger & Cilantro

Ingredients:

- ½ cup of tamarind paste
- ¼ cup of jaggery or brown sugar
- 2 tablespoons of grated ginger
- 2 cloves of garlic
- 2 green chilies
- ¼ cup of cilantro, chopped
- Salt to taste

Instructions:

1. In a pan, combine the tamarind paste, jaggery, ginger, garlic, green chilies, and salt. Bring to a boil and simmer for 10-15 minutes.
2. Remove from heat and let it cool.
3. Once cooled, blend the mixture in a blender until smooth.
4. Stir in the cilantro and serve with dosa, idli, or as a dip.

Cumin & Coriander Roasted Cauliflower with Yogurt & Mint Chutney

Ingredients:

- 1 head of cauliflower, cut into florets
- 2 tablespoons olive oil
- 1 teaspoon cumin powder
- 1 teaspoon coriander powder

- Salt and pepper to taste
- 1 cup of plain yogurt
- 2 tablespoons mint chutney

Instructions:

1. Preheat oven to 375F.
2. In a large bowl, combine the cauliflower florets, olive oil, cumin powder, coriander powder, salt and pepper. Mix well.
3. Spread the cauliflower mixture on a baking sheet and bake for 20-25 minutes, or until tender.
4. Take out of the oven and let it cool.
5. Serve warm, topped with a dollop of yogurt and mint chutney on top.

Chickpea & Spinach Curry with Turmeric & Cumin

Ingredients:

- 2 tablespoons olive oil
- 1 onion, diced
- 2 cloves of garlic, minced
- 1 teaspoon turmeric powder
- 1 teaspoon cumin powder
- 1 can of chickpeas, drained and rinsed
- 2 cups of spinach, washed and chopped
- Salt and pepper to taste
- 1 cup of water
- 2 tablespoons chopped cilantro

Instructions:

1. Heat the olive oil in a pan over medium heat.
2. Add the onion and garlic, sauté for 2-3 minutes.
3. Add the turmeric powder and cumin powder, sauté for another 2-3 minutes.
4. Add the chickpeas, spinach, salt, pepper, and water. Bring to a boil and then reduce heat to low and let it simmer for 10-15 minutes.
5. Taste and adjust seasoning as needed.
6. Stir in the cilantro. Serve warm with rice or naan bread.

Lentil & Vegetable Sambar with Tamarind & Mustard Seeds

Ingredients:

- 1 cup of lentils, soaked overnight
- 2 cups of mixed vegetables, diced (carrots, okra, eggplant, etc.)
- 1 teaspoon tamarind paste
- 1 teaspoon mustard seeds
- 1 teaspoon cumin powder
- Salt and pepper to taste
- 2 cups of water
- 2 tablespoons chopped cilantro

Instructions:

1. Drain the lentils and place them in a pan with water and bring to a boil.
2. Reduce heat to low and let it simmer for 15-20 minutes or until tender.
3. In a separate pan, heat some oil and add the mustard seeds. Once they start to pop, add the cumin powder, tamarind paste, salt, pepper, and vegetables.

4. Sauté for 2-3 minutes.
5. Add the cooked lentils and 2 cups of water. Bring to a boil and then reduce heat to low and let it simmer for another 10-15 minutes.
6. Taste and adjust seasoning as needed.
7. Stir in the cilantro. Serve warm with rice or dosa.

Ayurvedic Pickle with Lemon, Ginger & Mustard Seeds

Ingredients:

- 2 lemons, sliced
- 2 inches of ginger, sliced
- 2 tablespoons mustard seeds
- ¼ cup of olive oil
- Salt and pepper to taste
- 1 teaspoon cumin powder
- 1 teaspoon coriander powder

Instructions:

1. In a jar, combine the lemon slices, ginger slices, mustard seeds, olive oil, salt, pepper, cumin powder, and coriander powder. Mix well.
2. Let it sit for at least a day before using, for the flavors to meld together.
3. Store in the refrigerator for up to a month.
4. Serve as a condiment with rice, dosa, or as a sandwich spread.

Cumin & Turmeric Roasted Carrots with Yogurt & Cilantro Chutney

Ingredients:

- 2 cups of sliced carrots
- 2 tablespoons olive oil
- 1 teaspoon cumin powder
- 1 teaspoon turmeric powder
- Salt and pepper to taste
- 1 cup of plain yogurt
- 2 tablespoons cilantro chutney

Instructions:

1. Pre-Heat oven to 375F.
2. In a large bowl, combine the sliced carrots, olive oil, cumin powder, turmeric powder, salt and pepper. Mix well.
3. Spread the carrot mixture on a baking sheet and bake for 20-25 minutes, or until tender.
4. Take out of the oven and let it cool.
5. Serve warm, topped with a dollop of yogurt and cilantro chutney on top.

Spinach & Fenugreek Chutney with Coconut & Lime

Ingredients:

- 2 cups of spinach, washed and chopped
- 1 cup of fenugreek leaves, washed and chopped
- ½ cup of grated coconut
- 2 cloves of garlic
- ¼ cup of water
- Juice of 1 lime
- Salt and pepper to taste

Instructions:

1. In a food processor, combine the spinach, fenugreek leaves, coconut, garlic, water, lime juice, salt, and pepper. Pulse until smooth.
2. Taste and adjust seasoning as needed.
3. Serve as a dip or spread on sandwiches or as a side dish.

Lentil & Vegetable Dhokla with Cumin & Coriander

Ingredients:

- 1 cup of lentils, soaked overnight
- 2 cups of mixed vegetables, grated (carrots, zucchini, cabbage)
- 1 teaspoon cumin powder
- 1 teaspoon coriander powder
- Salt and pepper to taste
- 1 teaspoon baking powder
- ¼ cup of yogurt
- 2 tablespoons chopped cilantro

Instructions:

1. Drain the lentils and place them in a blender. Add 1 cup of water and blend until smooth.
2. In a large mixing bowl, combine the lentil mixture, vegetables, cumin powder, coriander powder, salt and pepper, baking powder, and yogurt. Mix well.
3. Taste and adjust seasoning as needed.
4. Grease a dhokla or cake pan and pour the mixture into it.
5. Steam for 15-20 minutes or until cooked through.
6. Once cool, remove from the pan and cut into squares.

7. Garnish with cilantro and serve with tamarind or mint chutney.

Ayurvedic Dipping Sauce with Tamarind, Cumin & Coriander
Ingredients:

- ½ cup of tamarind paste
- 2 tablespoons of grated ginger
- 2 cloves of garlic
- 2 green chilies
- 1 teaspoon cumin powder
- 1 teaspoon coriander powder
- Salt to taste

Instructions:

1. In a pan, combine the tamarind paste, ginger, garlic, green chilies, cumin powder, coriander powder, and salt.
2. Heat the mixture over medium heat, stirring constantly, until it becomes thick and bubbly.
3. Let it cool and then transfer to a blender or food processor. Pulse until smooth.
4. Serve as a dipping sauce for samosas, dosa, or idli. Can also be used as a marinade for meats or vegetables.

Cumin & Coriander Roasted Beets with Yogurt & Mint Chutney
Ingredients:

- 2 cups of diced beets
- 2 tablespoons olive oil
- 1 teaspoon cumin powder

- 1 teaspoon coriander powder
- Salt and pepper to taste
- 1 cup of plain yogurt
- 2 tablespoons mint chutney

Instructions:

1. Preheat oven to 375F.
2. In a large bowl, combine the diced beets, olive oil, cumin powder, coriander powder, salt and pepper. Mix well.
3. Spread the beet mixture on a baking sheet and bake for 20-25 minutes, or until tender.
4. Take out of the oven and let it cool.
5. Serve warm, topped with a dollop of yogurt and mint chutney on top.

Chickpea & Spinach Curry with Coconut Milk & Lemongrass
Ingredients:

- 2 tablespoons olive oil
- 1 onion, diced
- 2 cloves of garlic, minced
- 1 teaspoon turmeric powder
- 1 teaspoon cumin powder
- 1 can of chickpeas, drained and rinsed
- 2 cups of spinach, washed and chopped
- 1 cup of coconut milk
- 1 stalk of lemongrass, bruised
- Salt and pepper to taste
- 2 tablespoons chopped cilantro

Instructions:

1. Heat the olive oil in a pan over medium heat.
2. Add the onion and garlic, sauté for 2-3 minutes.
3. Add the turmeric powder and cumin powder, sauté for another 2-3 minutes.
4. Add the chickpeas, spinach, coconut milk, lemongrass, salt, pepper, and bring to a boil.
5. Reduce heat to low and let it simmer for 10-15 minutes.
6. Taste and adjust seasoning as needed.
7. Stir in the cilantro. Serve warm with rice or naan bread.

Lentil & Vegetable Idli with Coconut & Mustard Seeds

Ingredients:

- 1 cup of lentils, soaked overnight
- 2 cups of mixed vegetables, grated (carrots, zucchini, cabbage)
- ½ cup of grated coconut
- 1 teaspoon mustard seeds
- Salt and pepper to taste
- 1 teaspoon baking powder
- ¼ cup of yogurt
- 2 tablespoons chopped cilantro

Instructions:

1. Drain the lentils and place them in a blender. Add 1 cup of water and blend until smooth.
2. In a large mixing bowl, combine the lentil mixture, vegetables, coconut, mustard seeds, salt and pepper, baking powder, and yogurt. Mix well.

3. Taste and adjust seasoning as needed.
4. Grease an idli or muffin pan and pour the mixture into it.
5. Steam for 15-20 minutes or until cooked through.
6. Once cool, remove from the pan and cut into squares.
7. Garnish with cilantro and serve with coconut chutney or sambar.

Ayurvedic Chutney with Cilantro, Ginger & Lime

Ingredients:

- 2 cups of cilantro, washed and chopped
- ¼ cup of grated ginger
- 2 cloves of garlic
- Juice of 2 limes
- Salt and pepper to taste

Instructions:

1. In a food processor, combine the cilantro, ginger, garlic, lime juice, salt, and pepper. Pulse until smooth.
2. Taste and adjust seasoning as needed.
3. Serve as a dip or spread on sandwiches or as a side dish.

CHAPTER 6: APPETIZERS AND SNACKS

Samosas with Tamarind & Cilantro Chutney

Ingredients:

- 1 cup all-purpose flour
- ¼ cup ghee
- ¼ tsp salt
- ½ cup water
- 1 cup mashed potatoes
- ½ cup peas
- ¼ tsp cumin powder
- ¼ tsp coriander powder
- ¼ tsp red chili powder
- ¼ tsp garam masala powder
- ¼ cup tamarind chutney
- ¼ cup cilantro chutney

Instructions:

1. In a mixing bowl, combine the flour, ghee, and salt. Mix well.
2. Slowly add water while kneading the dough until it becomes smooth and pliable.
3. Cover and set aside for 30 minutes.
4. In a separate pan, sauté the mashed potatoes and peas with cumin, coriander, red chili, and garam masala powder.

5. Roll out the dough into small circles and fill with the potato and pea mixture.
6. Fry the samosas in oil until golden brown.
7. Serve hot with tamarind and cilantro chutney.

Lentil Fritters with Turmeric & Cumin
Ingredients:

- 1 cup split red lentils
- ¼ tsp salt
- ¼ tsp turmeric powder
- ¼ tsp cumin powder
- ¼ tsp red chili powder
- ¼ cup water
- Oil for frying

Instructions:

1. Soak the lentils in water for 2 hours.
2. Drain and grind the lentils into a fine paste.
3. Add salt, turmeric, cumin, red chili powder, and water. Mix well.
4. Heat oil in a pan and drop spoonfuls of the batter into the oil.
5. Fry until golden brown.
6. Drain on paper towels and serve hot.

Spiced Almonds with Ginger & Cardamom
Ingredients:

- 1 cup raw almonds
- 1 tsp ghee

- ¼ tsp ginger powder
- ¼ tsp cardamom powder
- ¼ tsp salt

Instructions:

1. In a pan, heat the ghee and add the almonds.
2. Roast the almonds until golden brown.
3. Add ginger, cardamom, and salt. Mix well.
4. Serve as a snack or garnish for desserts.

Vegetable & Lentil Kachori with Tamarind & Cilantro Chutney

Ingredients:

- 1 cup all-purpose flour
- ¼ cup ghee
- ¼ tsp salt
- ½ cup water
- 1 cup mashed potatoes
- ½ cup peas
- ¼ tsp cumin powder
- ¼ tsp coriander powder
- ¼ tsp red chili powder
- ¼ cup tamarind chutney
- ¼ cup cilantro chutney
- Oil for frying

Instructions:

1. In a mixing bowl, combine the flour, ghee, and salt. Mix well.

2. Slowly add water while kneading the dough until it becomes smooth and pliable.
3. Cover and set aside for 30 minutes.
4. In a separate pan, sauté the mashed potatoes and peas with cumin, coriander, red chili powder.
5. Roll out the dough into small circles and fill with the potato and pea mixture.
6. Fry the kachoris in oil until golden brown.
7. Serve hot with tamarind and cilantro chutney.

Ayurvedic Popcorn with Ghee, Turmeric & Salt
Ingredients:

- ¼ cup popcorn kernels
- 1 tbsp ghee
- ¼ tsp turmeric powder
- ¼ tsp salt

Instructions:

1. Heat ghee in a pan and add the popcorn kernels.
2. Cover and wait for the kernels to pop.
3. Once the popcorn is done, remove from heat and add turmeric and salt.
4. Mix well and serve as a snack.

Cumin & Coriander Roasted Chickpeas with Lime & Parsley
Ingredients:

- 1 cup chickpeas (cooked)
- 1 tsp ghee

- ¼ tsp cumin powder
- ¼ tsp coriander powder
- ¼ tsp salt
- 1 tbsp lime juice
- 1 tbsp chopped parsley

Instructions:

1. Preheat oven to 375°F (190°C).
2. In a mixing bowl, combine the chickpeas, ghee, cumin, coriander, and salt.
3. Spread the chickpeas on a baking sheet and roast for 15-20 minutes.
4. Once done, remove from oven and add lime juice and parsley.
5. Mix well and serve as a snack or garnish for salads.

Lentil & Vegetable Dhokla with Tamarind & Cilantro Chutney

Ingredients:

- 1 cup split chickpeas
- ¼ cup grated carrots
- ¼ cup grated zucchini
- ¼ tsp salt
- ¼ tsp turmeric powder
- ¼ tsp cumin powder
- ¼ tsp red chili powder
- ¼ cup tamarind chutney
- ¼ cup cilantro chutney
- Oil for frying

Instructions:

1. Soak the chickpeas overnight and grind them into a fine paste.
2. In a mixing bowl, combine the ground chickpeas, grated vegetables, salt, turmeric, cumin, and red chili powder.
3. Mix well and let the batter sit for 20 minutes.
4. Grease a steaming plate and pour the batter into it.
5. Steam for 20 minutes or until a toothpick inserted comes out clean.
6. Once done, remove from heat and cut into squares.
7. Fry the dhoklas in oil until golden brown
8. Serve hot with tamarind and cilantro chutney.

Ayurvedic Trail Mix with Nuts, Seeds & Dried Fruits
Ingredients:

- ½ cup roasted almonds
- ½ cup roasted cashews
- ½ cup pumpkin seeds
- ½ cup sunflower seeds
- ½ cup dried cranberries
- ½ cup dried apricots
- ¼ tsp ginger powder
- ¼ tsp cardamom powder
- ¼ tsp salt

Instructions:

1. In a mixing bowl, combine all the ingredients.
2. Mix well and store in an airtight container.
3. Serve as a snack or garnish for desserts.

Cumin & Turmeric Roasted Peanuts with Lime & Cilantro

Ingredients:

- 1 cup raw peanuts
- 1 tsp ghee
- ¼ tsp cumin powder
- ¼ tsp turmeric powder
- ¼ tsp salt
- 1 tbsp lime juice
- 1 tbsp chopped cilantro

Instructions:

1. Preheat oven to 375°F (190°C).
2. In a mixing bowl, combine the peanuts, ghee, cumin, turmeric, and salt.
3. Spread the peanuts on a baking sheet and roast for 15-20 minutes.
4. Once done, remove from oven and add lime juice and cilantro.
5. Mix well and serve as a snack or garnish for salads.

Chickpea & Spinach Cutlets with Cumin & Coriander

Ingredients:

- 1 cup cooked chickpeas
- 1 cup chopped spinach
- ¼ tsp cumin powder
- ¼ tsp coriander powder
- ¼ tsp red chili powder

- ¼ tsp salt
- ¼ cup flour
- Oil for frying

Instructions:

1. In a mixing bowl, combine the chickpeas, spinach, cumin, coriander, red chili powder, and salt.
2. Mash the mixture and form small cutlets.
3. Roll the cutlets in flour.
4. Fry the cutlets in oil until golden brown.
5. Serve hot as a snack or appetizer.

Lentil & Vegetable Bonda with Tamarind & Mustard Seeds
Ingredients:

- 1 cup split black lentils
- ½ cup grated carrots
- ½ cup grated zucchini
- ¼ tsp salt
- ¼ tsp turmeric powder
- ¼ tsp cumin powder
- ¼ tsp red chili powder
- ¼ cup tamarind chutney
- 1 tsp mustard seeds
- Oil for frying

Instructions:

1. Soak the lentils overnight and grind them into a fine paste.

2. In a mixing bowl, combine the ground lentils, grated vegetables, salt, turmeric, cumin, and red chili powder.
3. Mix well and let the batter sit for 20 minutes.
4. Grease your hands and form small balls from the batter.
5. Heat oil in a pan and add mustard seeds. Once they crackle, add the bondas.
6. Fry the bondas until golden brown.
7. Serve hot with tamarind chutney.

Ayurvedic Chutney with Lime, Ginger & Mustard Seeds

Ingredients:

- ½ cup lime juice
- ¼ cup chopped cilantro
- ¼ cup chopped mint
- ¼ tsp ginger powder
- ¼ tsp cumin powder
- ¼ tsp salt
- 1 tsp mustard seeds

Instructions:

1. In a mixing bowl, combine all the ingredients.
2. Mix well and store in an airtight container.
3. Serve as a dip or condiment for appetizers and main dishes.

Cumin & Coriander Roasted Cashews with Yogurt & Mint Chutney

Ingredients:

- 1 cup cashews
- 1 tsp ghee

- ¼ tsp cumin powder
- ¼ tsp coriander powder
- ¼ tsp salt
- ¼ cup plain yogurt
- ¼ cup mint chutney

Instructions:

1. Preheat oven to 375°F (190°C).
2. In a mixing bowl, combine the cashews, ghee, cumin, coriander, and salt.
3. Spread the cashews on a baking sheet and roast for 15-20 minutes.
4. Once done, remove from oven and add yogurt and mint chutney.
5. Mix well and serve as a snack or garnish for salads.

Spinach & Fenugreek Samosas with Tamarind & Cilantro Chutney
Ingredients:

- 1 cup all-purpose flour
- ¼ cup ghee
- ¼ tsp salt
- ½ cup water
- 1 cup chopped spinach
- ¼ cup chopped fenugreek leaves
- ¼ tsp cumin powder
- ¼ tsp coriander powder
- ¼ tsp red chili powder
- ¼ cup tamarind chutney
- ¼ cup cilantro chutney

- Oil for frying

Instructions:

1. In a mixing bowl, combine the flour, ghee, and salt. Mix well.
2. Slowly add water while kneading the dough until it becomes smooth and pliable.
3. Cover and set aside for 30 minutes.
4. In a separate pan, sauté the spinach and fenugreek leaves with cumin, coriander, and red chili powder.
5. Roll out the dough into small circles and fill with the spinach and fenugreek mixture.
6. Fry the samosas in oil until golden brown.
7. Serve hot with tamarind and cilantro chutney.

Lentil & Vegetable Samosas with Tamarind & Cilantro Chutney
Ingredients:

- 1 cup all-purpose flour
- ¼ cup ghee
- ¼ tsp salt
- ½ cup water
- 1 cup mashed lentils
- ½ cup grated vegetables (carrots, zucchini, etc)
- ¼ tsp cumin powder
- ¼ tsp coriander powder
- ¼ tsp red chili powder
- ¼ cup tamarind chutney
- ¼ cup cilantro chutney
- Oil for frying

Instructions:

1. In a mixing bowl, combine the flour, ghee, and salt. Mix well.
2. Slowly add water while kneading the dough until it becomes smooth and pliable.
3. Cover and set aside for 30 minutes. In a separate pan, sauté the grated vegetables with cumin, coriander, and red chili powder.
4. Mix in the mashed lentils and stir well.
5. Roll out the dough into small circle and fill with the lentil and vegetable mixture.
6. Fry the samosas in oil until golden brown.
7. Serve hot with tamarind and cilantro chutney.

Ayurvedic Spiced Nuts with Turmeric, Cumin & Coriander

Ingredients:

- 1 cup mixed nuts (almonds, cashews, walnuts)
- 1 tsp ghee
- ¼ tsp turmeric powder
- ¼ tsp cumin powder
- ¼ tsp coriander powder
- ¼ tsp salt

Instructions:

1. In a mixing bowl, combine the nuts, ghee, turmeric, cumin, coriander, and salt.
2. Spread the nuts on a baking sheet and roast for 15-20 minutes.
3. Once done, remove from oven and let it cool.
4. Serve as a snack or garnish for desserts.

Cumin & Turmeric Roasted Pistachios with Lime & Parsley

Ingredients:

- 1 cup pistachios
- 1 tsp ghee
- ¼ tsp cumin powder
- ¼ tsp turmeric powder
- ¼ tsp salt
- 1 tbsp lime juice
- 1 tbsp chopped parsley

Instructions:

1. Preheat oven to 375°F (190°C).
2. In a mixing bowl, combine the pistachios, ghee, cumin, turmeric, and salt.
3. Spread the pistachios on a baking sheet and roast for 15-20 minutes.
4. Once done, remove from oven and add lime juice and parsley.
5. Mix well and serve as a snack or garnish for salads.

Chickpea & Spinach Vada with Cumin & Coriander

Ingredients:

- 1 cup cooked chickpeas
- 1 cup chopped spinach
- ¼ tsp cumin powder
- ¼ tsp coriander powder
- ¼ tsp red chili powder

- ¼ tsp salt
- ¼ cup flour
- Oil for frying

Instructions:

1. In a mixing bowl, combine the chickpeas, spinach, cumin, coriander, red chili powder, salt,and flour.
2. Mash the mixture and form small vadas.
3. Fry the vadas in oil until golden brown.
4. Serve hot as a snack or appetizer.

Lentil & Vegetable Kebabs with Turmeric & Cumin
Ingredients:

- 1 cup split black lentils
- ½ cup grated vegetables (carrots, zucchini, etc)
- ¼ tsp salt
- ¼ tsp turmeric powder
- ¼ tsp cumin powder
- ¼ tsp red chili powder
- ¼ cup yogurt
- Oil for grilling

Instructions:

1. Soak the lentils overnight and grind them into a fine paste.
2. In a mixing bowl, combine the ground lentils, grated vegetables, salt, turmeric, cumin, red chili powder, and yogurt.
3. Mix well and let the batter sit for 20 minutes.

4. Grease your hands and form small kebab shapes from the batter.
5. Heat oil in a pan and grill the kebabs until fully cooked.
6. Serve hot as a main dish or appetizer.

Ayurvedic Yogurt Dip with Cumin, Coriander & Lime

Ingredients:

- 1 cup plain yogurt
- ¼ tsp cumin powder
- ¼ tsp coriander powder
- 1/4 tsp salt
- 1 tbsp lime juice
- 1 tbsp chopped cilantro

Instructions:

1. In a mixing bowl, combine the yogurt, cumin, coriander, salt, lime juice, and cilantro.
2. Mix well and store in an airtight container.
3. Serve as a dip or condiment for appetizers and main dishes.

CHAPTER 7: DESSERTS AND BEVERAGES

Cardamom & Pistachio Ice Cream with Rosewater

Ingredients:

- 2 cups heavy cream
- 1 can of full-fat coconut milk
- 1 cup of sugar
- 1 tablespoon of cardamom powder
- 1 teaspoon of rosewater
- 1 cup of chopped pistachios

Instructions:

1. In a saucepan, combine the heavy cream, coconut milk and sugar. Heat the mixture over medium heat, stirring constantly, until the sugar has dissolved.
2. Remove the pan from heat and add the cardamom powder and rosewater. Stir to combine.
3. Allow the mixture to cool completely before transferring it to an ice cream maker and churning it according to the manufacturer's instructions.
4. Once the ice cream is churned, fold in the chopped pistachios.
5. Transfer the ice cream to a container and freeze it for at least 4 hours or until firm.

Rosewater & Saffron Pudding with Pistachios

Ingredients:

- 1 cup of sugar
- 1 cup of cornstarch
- 1 teaspoon of saffron strands
- 1 teaspoon of rosewater
- 2 cups of milk
- 1 cup of chopped pistachios

Instructions:

1. In a saucepan, combine the sugar, cornstarch, saffron strands, and rosewater. Stir until well combined.
2. Gradually add the milk, stirring constantly, until the mixture is smooth.
3. Cook the mixture over medium heat, stirring constantly, until it thickens.
4. Remove the pan from heat and transfer the pudding to a bowl. Allow it to cool completely. Once the pudding is cooled, fold in the chopped pistachios.
5. Serve the pudding in individual bowls and refrigerate until ready to serve.

Ginger & Turmeric Tea with Honey & Lime

Ingredients:

- 4 cups of water
- 1-inch piece of ginger, grated
- 1 teaspoon of turmeric powder
- 1 teaspoon of honey
- Juice of 1 lime

Instructions:

1. In a pot, bring the water to a boil.
2. Add the grated ginger, turmeric powder, and stir to combine.
3. Reduce the heat and allow the tea to simmer for 5 minutes.
4. Remove the pot from heat and strain the tea.
5. Stir in the honey and lime juice.
6. Serve the tea warm or chilled, as desired.

Mango & Cardamom Sorbet with Coconut Milk

Ingredients:

- 2 cups of fresh mango puree
- 1 can of full-fat coconut milk
- 1 cup of sugar
- 1 teaspoon of cardamom powder
- 1 tablespoon of lime juice

Instructions:

1. In a saucepan, combine the mango puree, coconut milk, sugar, and cardamom powder. Heat the mixture over medium heat, stirring constantly, until the sugar has dissolved.
2. Remove the pan from heat and stir in the lime juice. Allow the mixture to cool completely.
3. Transfer the mixture to an ice cream maker and churn it according to the manufacturer's instructions.
4. Once the sorbet is churned, transfer it to a container and freeze it for at least 4 hours or until firm.

Ayurvedic Sweet Lassi with Rosewater & Pistachios

Ingredients:

- 2 cups of plain yogurt
- 1 cup of cold water
- ¼ cup of sugar
- 1 teaspoon of rosewater
- ¼ cup of chopped pistachios

Instructions:

1. In a blender, combine the yogurt, water, sugar and rosewater. Blend until smooth.
2. Transfer the lassi to a glass and garnish with chopped pistachios.
3. Serve chilled and enjoy!

Cumin & Coriander Roasted Apples with Yogurt & Cinnamon

Ingredients:

- 4 apples, peeled and cored
- 2 tablespoons of ghee or coconut oil
- 1 teaspoon of cumin powder
- 1 teaspoon of coriander powder
- 1 teaspoon of cinnamon powder
- 1 cup of plain yogurt

Instructions:

1. Preheat the oven to 400°F (200°C).

2. In a small bowl, mix together the ghee or coconut oil, cumin powder, coriander powder, and cinnamon powder.
3. Cut the apples into wedges and toss them in the spice mixture.
4. Arrange the apples on a baking sheet and bake for 20-25 minutes, or until tender and golden brown.
5. Serve the apples warm with a dollop of yogurt.

Lentil & Vegetable Kheer with Cardamom & Saffron

Ingredients:

- 1 cup of red lentils
- 2 cups of water
- 1 cup of mixed vegetables (carrots, peas, green beans)
- 1 can of full-fat coconut milk
- 1 cup of sugar
- 1 teaspoon of cardamom powder
- 1 teaspoon of saffron strands
- ¼ cup of chopped cashews (optional)

Instructions:

1. In a pot, combine the lentils, water, and vegetables. Bring the mixture to a boil and then reduce the heat and allow it to simmer for 15 minutes or until the lentils are cooked through.
2. Add the coconut milk, sugar, cardamom powder, and saffron strands. Stir to combine.
3. Allow the kheer to simmer for an additional 5 minutes.
4. Remove the pot from heat and transfer the kheer to a bowl. Allow it to cool completely.

5. Once the kheer is cooled, garnish with chopped cashews (if desired) and serve chilled.

Ayurvedic Spiced Coffee with Ginger & Cardamom
Ingredients:

- 2 cups of strong brewed coffee
- 1 teaspoon of ginger powder
- 1 teaspoon of cardamom powder
- 1 teaspoon of honey1 tablespoon of ghee or coconut oil

Instructions:

1. In a small saucepan, combine the coffee, ginger powder, cardamom powder, and honey. Heat the mixture over medium heat, stirring constantly, until heated through.
2. Remove the pan from heat and stir in the ghee or coconut oil.
3. Serve the coffee warm and enjoy the unique and delicious Ayurvedic twist on a classic beverage.

Cumin & Turmeric Roasted Pears with Yogurt & Honey
Ingredients:

- 4 pears, peeled and cored
- 2 tablespoons of ghee or coconut oil
- 1 teaspoon of cumin powder
- 1 teaspoon of turmeric powder
- 1 cup of plain yogurt
- 1 teaspoon of honey

Instructions:

1. Preheat the oven to 400°F (200°C).
2. In a small bowl, mix together the ghee or coconut oil, cumin powder, and turmeric powder.
3. Cut the pears into wedges and toss them in the spice mixture.
4. Arrange the pears on a baking sheet and bake for 20-25 minutes, or until tender and golden brown.
5. Serve the pears warm with a dollop of yogurt and a drizzle of honey.

Chickpea & Spinach Halwa with Ghee & Cardamom

Ingredients:

- 1 cup of chickpeas, soaked overnight and drained
- 1 cup of spinach, chopped
- 1 cup of ghee
- 1 cup of sugar
- 1 teaspoon of cardamom powder
- ¼ cup of chopped almonds (optional)

Instructions:

1. In a food processor, grind the chickpeas into a fine paste.
2. In a pan, heat the ghee and add the chickpea paste. Cook for 5-7 minutes or until the paste turns golden brown.
3. Add the spinach, sugar, and cardamom powder. Stir to combine.
4. Cook the mixture for an additional 5 minutes or until the spinach is wilted and the mixture is thick and sticky.

5. Remove the pan from heat and transfer the halwa to a bowl. Allow it to cool completely.
6. Once the halwa is cooled, garnish with chopped almonds (if desired) and serve chilled.

Lentil & Vegetable Payasam with Coconut Milk & Cardamom

Ingredients:

- 1 cup of red lentils
- 2 cups of water
- 1 cup of mixed vegetables (carrots, peas, green beans)
- 1 can of full-fat coconut milk
- 1 cup of jaggery or brown sugar
- 1 teaspoon of cardamom powder
- ¼ cup of chopped cashews (optional)

Instructions:

1. In a pot, combine the lentils, water, and vegetables. Bring the mixture to a boil and then reduce the heat and allow it to simmer for 15 minutes or until the lentils are cooked through.
2. Add the coconut milk, jaggery or brown sugar, cardamom powder. Stir to combine.
3. Allow the payasam to simmer for an additional 5 minutes.
4. Remove the pot from heat and transfer the payasam to a bowl. Allow it to cool completely.
5. Once the payasam is cooled, garnish with chopped cashews (if desired) and serve chilled.

Ayurvedic Rose Lassi with Pistachios & Cardamom

Ingredients:

- 2 cups of plain yogurt
- 1 cup of cold water
- ¼ cup of sugar
- 1 teaspoon of rosewater
- 1 teaspoon of cardamom powder
- ¼ cup of chopped pistachios

Instructions:

1. In a blender, combine the yogurt, water, sugar, rosewater, and cardamom powder. Blend until smooth.
2. Transfer the lassi to a glass and garnish with chopped pistachios.
3. Serve chilled and enjoy!

Cumin & Turmeric Roasted Plums with Yogurt & Honey

Ingredients:

- 4 plums, halved and pitted
- 2 tablespoons of ghee or coconut oil
- 1 teaspoon of cumin powder
- 1 teaspoon of turmeric powder
- 1 cup of plain yogurt
- 1 teaspoon of honey

Instructions:

1. Preheat the oven to 400°F (200°C).

2. In a small bowl, mix together the ghee or coconut oil, cumin powder, and turmeric powder.
3. Toss the plums in the spice mixture and place them cut side up on a baking sheet.
4. Roast the plums for 20-25 minutes, or until tender and golden brown.
5. Serve the plums warm with a dollop of yogurt and a drizzle of honey.

Chickpea & Spinach Kheer with Cardamom & Saffron

Ingredients:

- 1 cup of chickpeas, soaked overnight and drained
- 1 cup of spinach, chopped
- 2 cups of water
- 1 cup of sugar
- 1 teaspoon of cardamom powder
- 1 teaspoon of saffron strands
- ¼ cup of chopped cashews (optional)

Instructions:

1. In a pot, combine the chickpeas, spinach, water, sugar, cardamom powder, and saffron strands. Bring the mixture to a boil and then reduce the heat and allow it to simmer for 15 minutes or until the chickpeas are cooked through.
2. Remove the pot from heat and transfer the kheer to a bowl. Allow it to cool completely.
3. Once the kheer is cooled, garnish with chopped cashews (if desired) and serve chilled.

Lentil & Vegetable Phirni with Rosewater & Pistachios

Ingredients:

- 1 cup of red lentils
- 2 cups of water
- 1 cup of mixed vegetables (carrots, peas, green beans)
- 1 cup of milk
- 1 cup of sugar
- 1 teaspoon of rosewater
- ¼ cup of chopped pistachios

Instructions:

1. In a pot, combine the lentils, water, and vegetables. Bring the mixture to a boil and then reduce the heat and allow it to simmer for 15 minutes or until the lentils are cooked through.
2. Add the milk, sugar, and rosewater. Stir to combine.
3. Allow the phirni to simmer for an additional 5 minutes.
4. Remove the pot from heat and transfer the phirni to a bowl. Allow it to cool completely.
5. Once the phirni is cooled, garnish with chopped pistachios and serve chilled.

Ayurvedic Spiced Milk with Turmeric, Ginger & Cardamom

Ingredients:

- 2 cups of milk
- 1 teaspoon of turmeric powder
- 1 teaspoon of ginger powder
- 1 teaspoon of cardom powder
- 1 tablespoon of honey

- ¼ cup of chopped almonds (optional)

Instructions:

1. In a small saucepan, combine the milk, turmeric powder, ginger powder, cardamom powder, and honey. Heat the mixture over medium heat, stirring constantly, until heated through.
2. Remove the pan from heat and transfer the spiced milk to a glass.
3. Garnish with chopped almonds (if desired) and serve warm.

CHAPTER 8: SEASONAL INGREDIENT GUIDE

Meal planning and shopping list

Meal planning is an important aspect of following an Ayurvedic diet. It helps ensure that you have the right ingredients on hand to create nourishing and balanced meals that support your unique body type and health needs.

Here are some tips for creating an effective meal plan:

Identify your Ayurvedic body type: Before you start planning your meals, it's important to understand your Ayurvedic body type, also known as dosha, which will guide you in choosing the right foods for your body.

Plan your meals: Once you understand your body type, start planning your meals for the week. Make sure to include a variety of ingredients that support your dosha and include a balance of protein, healthy fats, and complex carbohydrates.

Include a variety of foods: Eating a variety of foods ensures that you get all the necessary nutrients your body needs.

Cook in bulk: Cook in bulk and freeze meals for later. This makes meal preparation easier and saves time.

Make a shopping list: Once you have your meals planned, make a list of all the ingredients you'll need for the week. Be sure to include pantry staples such as spices, oils, and condiments as well as fresh fruits, vegetables, and proteins.

Shop seasonally: When possible, try to shop for ingredients that are in season as they tend to be fresher and more nutrient-dense.

Keep it simple: Remember that the key to success is to keep your meals simple and easy to prepare.

Try to buy organic and non-GMO ingredients

By following these tips, you can create a meal plan that will help you stay on track with your Ayurvedic diet and make it easy to create nourishing and delicious meals at home.

Here is a sample shopping list for an Ayurvedic diet:

Produce:

Leafy greens (spinach, kale, collard greens)

Root vegetables (sweet potatoes, beets, carrots)

Squash (pumpkin, zucchini, butternut)

Berries (strawberries, blueberries, raspberries)

Melons (cantaloupe, honeydew)

Fruits (apples, pears, plums)

Herbs (cilantro, mint, parsley)

Spices (ginger, turmeric, cumin, coriander, cinnamon, cardamom)

Whole Grains (brown rice, quinoa, millet, barley)

Protein:

Chicken

Beef

Fish

Eggs

Tofu

Lentils

Chickpeas

Dairy:

Ghee

Milk

Yogurt

Cheese

Oils:

Coconut oil

Ghee

Sesame oil

Olive oil

Flaxseed oil

Nuts and Seeds:

Almonds

Walnuts

Cashews

Pistachios

Flaxseeds

Sunflower seeds

Herbs and Spices:

Turmeric

Cumin

Coriander

Cardamom

Cinnamon

Black pepper

Cloves

Ayurvedic Lifestyle Tips

An Ayurvedic lifestyle is not just about the food you eat but also about the way you live. Here are some tips for incorporating Ayurvedic principles into your daily life:

Wake up early: Wake up before sunrise and start your day with a glass of warm water and some light stretching.

Practice yoga and meditation: Yoga and meditation are great ways to balance the mind and body.

Get regular exercise: Regular exercise helps to balance the doshas and keep your body strong and healthy.

Avoid processed foods: Processed foods are not part of an Ayurvedic lifestyle.

Eat mindfully: Eating mindfully means paying attention to your food, savoring the flavors, and eating slowly.

Get enough sleep: Aim for 7-8 hours of sleep each night to help your body and mind rejuvenate.

Spend time in nature: Spending time in nature is calming and grounding, which helps to balance the doshas.

Practice self-care: Self-care is important for maintaining balance in the body and mind.

Connect with others: Connecting with others helps to balance the doshas and improve overall well-being.

Listen to your body: Listen to your body and pay attention to its needs. If you're feeling tired or stressed, take a break and rest.

By incorporating these tips into your daily life, you can create a more balanced and harmonious lifestyle that promotes optimal health and well-being.

CHAPTER 9: COMPREHENDING AYURVEDIC CULINARY ARTS

The Doshas And Individual Characteristics

Ayurveda, the ancient Indian system of medicine, recognizes three main body types, or doshas, which are known as **Vata, Pitta, and Kapha**. Each dosha is associated with a particular set of characteristics, and understanding these characteristics can help you determine your own dosha, and make lifestyle and diet choices that will help you achieve optimal health and well-being.

Vata dosha is associated with the elements of air and ether and is characterized by qualities such as dryness, lightness, and coldness. People with a predominance of Vata tend to be thin, energetic, and creative, but can also be prone to anxiety, dryness, and restlessness. To balance Vata, it is important to incorporate warm, nourishing, and grounding foods and lifestyle practices into your daily routine.

Pitta dosha is associated with the elements of fire and water and is characterized by qualities such as heat, sharpness, and oiliness. People with a predominance of Pitta tend to be sharp, competitive, and ambitious, but can also be prone to anger, inflammation, and skin issues. To balance Pitta, it is important to incorporate cooling, soothing, and calming foods and lifestyle practices into your daily routine.

Kapha dosha is associated with the elements of earth and water and is characterized by qualities such as density, weight, and moistness. People with a predominance of Kapha tend to be calm, stable, and loving, but can also be prone to sluggishness, congestion, and weight gain. To balance Kapha, it is important to incorporate light, stimulating, and warming foods and lifestyle practices into your daily routine.

It's important to note that everyone has all three doshas in their body, but one or two are usually more prominent, and understanding which dosha is dominant can help you make lifestyle and dietary choices that will help you achieve optimal health and well-being.

Eating according to your dosha, practicing yoga and meditation, and incorporating self-care practices such as oil massage, dry brushing, and daily routines, can help to balance the doshas. Additionally, it's important to pay attention to the emotional state, as emotional imbalances can also affect the doshas

The Impact Of Food Attributes On The Doshas

According to Ayurveda, the ancient Indian system of medicine, the qualities and attributes of food have a direct impact on the doshas, or body types, which are known as Vata, Pitta, and Kapha. Understanding these attributes and how they affect the doshas can help you make more informed choices about what to eat, and create a diet that is tailored to your unique body type and health needs.

Taste: Ayurveda recognizes six tastes – sweet, sour, salty, pungent, bitter, and astringent. Each taste has a specific effect on the doshas. For example, sweet, sour, and salty tastes tend to pacify Vata and Pitta, while pungent, bitter, and astringent tastes tend to pacify Kapha.

Temperature: Foods can also be classified based on their temperature, such as cold, cool, warm, or hot. Cold foods tend to pacify Pitta and Kapha, while warm foods tend to pacify Vata.

Post-Digestive Effect: Ayurveda also classifies foods based on their post-digestive effect, which refers to the effect that food has on the body after it has been digested. Some foods are considered to have a sweet post-digestive effect, which tends to pacify Vata and Pitta, while other foods are considered to have a sour or pungent post-digestive effect, which tends to pacify Kapha.

For example, for Vata dosha, which is associated with the elements of air and ether and is characterized by qualities such as dryness, lightness, and coldness, it's important to include warm, nourishing, and grounding foods such as soups, stews, and warm grains. On the other hand, for Pitta dosha, which is associated with the elements of fire and water and is characterized by qualities such as heat, sharpness, and oiliness, it's important to include cooling, soothing, and calming foods such as raw fruits and vegetables, and avoid spicy and oily foods.

Additionally, it's important to pay attention to the preparation method of food. For example, cooking food with ghee, a type of clarified butter, is considered to be grounding and nourishing for Vata, while using oils like coconut oil or olive oil is considered to be cooling and pacifying for Pitta.

Furthermore, the time of the day that food is consumed also plays a role in how it affects the doshas. For example, consuming heavy and dense foods at night can disrupt the Kapha dosha, which is associated with the elements of earth and water and is characterized by qualities such as density, weight, and moistness.

In conclusion, Ayurveda recognizes that the qualities and attributes of food have a direct impact on the doshas. By understanding the effects of taste, temperature, and post-digestive effect of food on the doshas, one can make more informed choices about what to eat, and create a diet that is tailored to their unique body

Ayurvedic Cooking Tips And Tricks

Here are some tips and tricks for incorporating Ayurvedic principles into your cooking:

Use natural and whole foods: Ayurvedic cooking encourages the use of natural and whole foods, such as fresh fruits and vegetables, whole grains, legumes, and nuts, as they are considered to be more nourishing and grounding than processed and refined foods.

Incorporate seasonal ingredients: Ayurvedic cooking encourages incorporating seasonal ingredients into meals as they are considered to be more nourishing and in tune with the body's natural rhythms. Eating seasonally can also help to reduce the environmental impact of food production.

Pay attention to the attributes and effects of food: Ayurvedic cooking involves paying attention to the attributes and effects of food on the doshas, such as taste, temperature, and post-digestive effect. By understanding the effects of food on the doshas, you can make more informed choices about what to eat and create a diet that is tailored to your unique body type and health needs.

Use ghee, ginger, and turmeric: Ghee, ginger, and turmeric are considered to be essential ingredients in Ayurvedic cooking as they are believed to have medicinal properties and can be used to balance the doshas. Ghee is considered to be grounding and nourishing for Vata, ginger is considered to be warming and stimulating for Kapha, and turmeric is considered to be cooling and soothing for Pitta.

Practice mindfulness while cooking and eating: Ayurvedic cooking encourages mindfulness while cooking and eating, such as paying attention to the colors, textures, and flavors of the food, and being present and mindful during the meal. This can help to promote balance and well-being.

Cook with love: Ayurvedic cooking encourages cooking with love and intention, as it's believed that food prepared with love and positive energy is more nourishing for the body and soul.

Experiment with herbs and spices: Ayurvedic cooking encourages the use of herbs and spices, as they are believed to have medicinal properties and can be used to balance the doshas. Some common Ayurvedic herbs and spices include cumin, coriander, cinnamon, cardamom, and black pepper.

Incorporate fermented foods: Ayurvedic cooking encourages incorporating fermented foods into meals, such as yogurt, kefir, and pickles, as they are believed to aid in digestion, and promote gut health.

By incorporating these tips and tricks into your cooking, you can create delicious and nourishing meals that are in tune with your unique body type and health needs, and promote optimal health and well-being.

How To Incorporate Ayurvedic Principles Into Your Daily Life

Start your day with a warm glass of water and lemon juice to aid in digestion and detoxification.

Incorporate daily meditation or yoga practice to promote balance and well-being.

Pay attention to the attributes and effects of food on the doshas, and make informed choices about what to eat based on your unique body type and health needs.

Incorporate seasonal and whole foods, herbs, and spices into your meals.

Incorporate fermented foods into your meals to promote gut health and aid in digestion.

Practice mindfulness while cooking and eating, paying attention to the colors, textures, and flavors of the food.

Prioritize good sleep and make sure you get enough rest.

Incorporate self-care practices, such as oil massage, herbal baths, and aromatherapy, to promote balance and well-being.

Listen to your body and give it the time it needs to rest and rejuvenate.

Seek guidance from Ayurvedic practitioners, who can provide personalized advice on how to incorporate Ayurvedic principles into your daily life.

By incorporating these principles into your daily life, you can promote optimal health and well-being and live in harmony with your unique body type. Remember that Ayurveda is a holistic system of medicine, and it's important to take a holistic approach to incorporating its principles into your daily life.

CONCLUSION

In conclusion, this Ayurvedic cookbook for westerners has provided an in-depth look at the ancient Indian system of medicine, Ayurveda, and how it can be applied to cooking and eating. By understanding the principles of Ayurvedic cooking and the attributes of food, readers can create delicious and nourishing meals that are tailored to their unique body type and health needs.

We have also discussed the importance of understanding the individual characteristics of each person and how they relate to the doshas. By understanding one's dosha, readers can make more informed choices about what to eat and create a diet that promotes optimal health and well-being. We also covered how to use this cookbook, including tips for meal planning, shopping, and incorporating Ayurvedic principles into daily life.

Additionally, we have highlighted the importance of mindfulness and positive energy in cooking and eating, as well as the importance of incorporating seasonal and whole foods, herbs and spices, and fermented foods into meals. We also emphasized the importance of incorporating Ayurvedic lifestyle practices, such as yoga and meditation, in addition to diet, to promote optimal health and well-being.

Finally, we have provided resources for further learning and inspiration, such as websites, books, and practitioners, for those who want to continue incorporating Ayurvedic principles into their lives. We encourage you to start incorporating Ayurvedic principles into your daily lives and to continue learning about the holistic system of medicine that is Ayurveda. By doing so, you'll be taking steps towards achieving optimal health and well-being.

RESOURCES FOR FURTHER LEARNING AND INSPIRATION

Books: "The Ayurvedic Cookbook" by Amadea Morningstar and Urmila Desai, "Healing with Whole Foods: Asian Traditions and Modern Nutrition" by Paul Pitchford, and "The Ayurvedic Kitchen: Cooking for Life" by Gail Tully.

Websites: The National Ayurvedic Medical Association (NAMA), Ayurvedic Institute, and The Ayurvedic Center for Healing Arts.

Online Courses: The Ayurveda Experience, Ayurveda Pura Academy, and The Ayurvedic Institute.

Podcasts: The Ayurvedic Medicine Podcast and Ayurveda for Modern Living Podcast

Community: Join Ayurvedic communities on social media such as Facebook, Instagram, and Meetup groups.

Practitioners: Consult with an Ayurvedic practitioner or doctor to get personalized advice on how to incorporate Ayurvedic principles into your daily life.

Yoga Centers: Look for local Ayurvedic Yoga centers, where you can learn and practice yoga under the guidance of an Ayurvedic practitioner.

By exploring these resources, you can deepen your understanding of Ayurveda, learn new recipes and techniques, and connect with other people who are interested in Ayurveda. You can also learn about Ayurveda's holistic approach to health and well-being, which can help you to take steps towards achieving optimal health and well-being.

ACKNOWLEDGMENTS AND CREDITS

I would like to extend my heartfelt gratitude to my loving husband and my amazing children, my two big boys and my precious little girl, for their unwavering support and encouragement throughout the writing process of this book. Their love and understanding have been a constant source of inspiration and motivation. Without their constant love and support, this book would not have been possible.

I would also like to thank my steadfast siblings for their unwavering support and encouragement. Their guidance, feedback, and support have been invaluable throughout the writing process, and I am grateful for their continued love and support.

I am truly blessed to have such a loving and supportive family, and I am forever grateful for their contributions to this book.

Thank you, my dear family, for being my rock, my inspiration, and my motivation. I love you all.

GLOSSARY OF AYURVEDIC TERMS

Agni – Digestive fire or metabolism.

Ama – Toxins that accumulate in the body due to poor digestion or an unhealthy lifestyle.

Doshas – The three energy types that govern the body and mind – Vata, Pitta, and Kapha.

Prakruti – The unique combination of doshas that make up an individual's constitution.

Tridoshic – A balance of all three doshas.

Vata – The dosha responsible for movement and circulation in the body.

Pitta – The dosha responsible for metabolism and digestion in the body.

Kapha – The dosha responsible for stability and structure in the body.

Sattva – The state of balance and harmony in the body and mind.

Ojas – The vital energy that nourishes the body and mind.

Prana – The vital energy that sustains the body and mind.

Rasayana – Ayurvedic rejuvenation therapy that promotes health and well-being.

Chakra – The energy centers in the body that govern different aspects of physical and mental well-being.

Marma – Vital points in the body that when stimulated, can promote healing and balance.

Ayurveda – The ancient Indian system of medicine that promotes health and well-being through the use of natural remedies and a holistic approach to healthcare.

Printed in Great Britain
by Amazon